PRAISE for God's Brothel

"[An] illuminating new book...."
    —CNN.com, August 1, 2004

"'Not a single woman [in a polygamous marriage] I've ever known is happy,' one polygamous wife says. Reading *God's Brothel*, you'll understand why."
    —*Denver Post*, August 15, 2004

"As *God's Brothel* makes clear, fundamentalist Mormon polygamy can lead to pedophilia, rape, domestic violence... incest and welfare fraud."
    —*Salt Lake Tribune*, August 15, 2004

"Highly recomended.... *God's Brothel* is a must read!"
    —The Center for Public Education and Information on Polygamy

"This book is a stinging indictment of the hidden practice of polygamy, in which patriarchy reaches an almost unfathomable extreme. The danger to women and children in this atmosphere is staggering and will shock many who consider the United States to be a beacon of freedom and champion of human rights. At the same time, these stories demonstrate the indomitable spirit that women often find within themselves to preserve their sense of self and that of their children."
    —Patricia Ireland, former president of the National Organization for Women

"Andrea Moore-Emmett has documented a gulag of Mormon fundamentalist and Christian polygamy whose female victims must daily choose between a dubious promise of redemption in exchange for a cruel and often violent life on earth. These are haunting stories of brave real life women who face impossible choices. Reading these I feel like a curious spectator to a gruesome accident ... these are not easy to read, but it's impossible to stop."
    —Frank Silverstein, former producer, CNN, CNBC

D0188660

Confirmed Mormon and Christian fundamentalist polygamists in North America

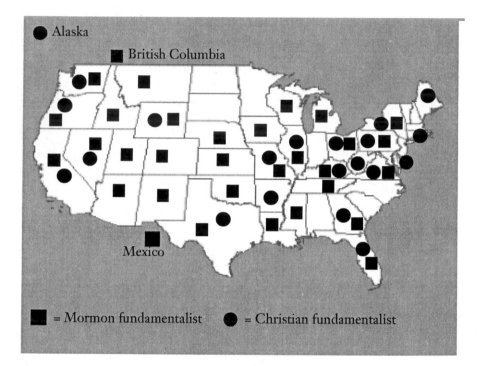

Note: The circles on the smaller states indicate Christian fundamentalist polygamists in Delaware and Massachusetts.

Andrea Moore-Emmett

God's Brothel

pince-nez press
san francisco

God's Brothel: The Extortion of Sex for Salvation in Contemporary Mormon and Christian Fundamentalist Polygamy and the Stories of 18 Women Who Escaped

Cover design: Bonnie Caldwell
Cover art: JoNell Evans, two panels of triptych "Pre-Ordained,"
from exhibit "Body Politics: An Artist's Journey in a Patriarchal
Society," Art Access Gallery, Salt Lake City, UT, March, 2004
Author photograph: Fred Hayes
See information on the artist on page 234
Fonts: Janson Test, Avant Garde, Luna ITC

Pince-Nez Press
San Francisco, CA
(415) 267-5978 fax (800) 579-3614
www.pince-nez.com
info@pince-nez.com

CONTENTS

PART ONE: Contemporary Polygamy in America

PART TWO: The Women Who Escaped

Polygamist groups/families from which the women escaped

Independent families in Utah and California including Tom Green	Vicky, Carmen, Allison
Apostolic United Brotherhood (Allred)	Lillian, Sylvia, Brenda
Patriarchal Christian Fellowship of God's Free Men and Women	Carmen
Church of the Firstborn of the Fullness of Time (LeBaron)	Janice
Latter-day Church of Christ (Kingston)	Connie, Stacy, Rowenna
True and Living Church of Jesus Christ of Saints of the Last Days (TLC)	Cindy
Fundamentalist Church of Jesus Christ of Latter-day Saints (FLDS)	Sherrie, Leona, Cora, Laura
The Righteous Branch	Wendy
Jesus Christ of United Order	Tammy
Church of the Lamb of God (Fred Collier)	Sarah

ACKNOWLEDGMENTS

So many individuals were essential to this process. Multitudes of thanks go to my publisher, Susan Vogel, who made this book a reality. It was a dream come true to have a publisher with the same vision for the book as I had.

Thank you is due to the artist, JoNell Evans, for lending her amazingly expressive artwork to the cover, and to the book designer, Bonnie Caldwell, for configuring the art and lettering so perfectly.

Thanks go to my ex-husband, Mark Emmett, for support, proofreading and untangling the computer glitches I so ably manage to "miscreate." Thanks also to my children, John, Erin and David, who are my biggest cheerleaders.

Much gratitude goes to Michael Kropveld for writing the insightful forward and for invaluable input, proofreading, perspective and encouragement. It proved to be critical to have someone unfamiliar with the Mormon and Christian fundamentalist polygamist cultures to carefully read through the manuscript. Though Michael was often swamped with his own work, he was generous with his time and meticulous in reading every word to assess what was being conveyed to a "non-Mormon speak" audience.

I am indebted to Richard S. Van Wagoner for his extensive research contained in his exhaustive book, *Mormon Polygamy, A History*, (Signature Books, 1989) which I have cited extensively. For those who want to go in depth on these issues, I recommend this book.

Thanks also to Charles Castle for assistance, encouragement and finding ways to make me laugh. Laughter was essential in keeping me sane while working on this project.

Thanks to Ed Cox for coining the phrase "Ecclesiastical Polygamy." Thanks go to Adam McKibbon for giving me the first ounce of recognition as to the merits of this work and for Koji Sakai for unfailing encouragement and belief in the power and importance of these stories. Thanks to Lorrie Casper for further computer help due to my being "the black hole of technology." Thanks also to Lynn Tempest, Ted Scheffler, Fred Hayes, Larry Gordley, Nicholas Claxton, Janja Lalich, Ron Loomis, Bernie Yee, Valeen Tippetts Avery and the many others who influenced, helped and encouraged me along the way. Thank you also to Bill Vogel, Ann Palmer, David Greenthal, Sherie Richmond and our artist friend for reviewing the manuscript. And to Julene Fisher and Jennifer Prunty for giving the manuscript one last read.

Last but not least, thanks go to the women who willingly poured out their painful stories to me and let me into their lives. It was exceedingly difficult for polygamy refugees to relive such debilitating memories, particularly since they have moved on with their lives and have worked hard to put their past behind them.

FOREWORD

This book comes at a very opportune time. The 2002 Winter Olympics held in Salt Lake City drew international attention to Utah, The Church of Jesus Christ of Latter-day Saints (Mormons) and to polygamy. Mormonism, one of the world's fastest growing religions, had its history, beliefs and practices profiled in numerous articles and TV programs. There is every indication that the Mormon Church would have undoubtedly preferred to have left out of the media spotlight the role of polygamy in the history of the church and its present day practice by fundamentalist Mormon groups and families.

In the media, members of polygamist groups described the positive experiences of the lifestyle and claimed the right to practice polygamy as an expression of their religious belief and as an individual choice. On the other hand, former members recounted the pain of their experiences in a culture they saw as rife with the physical and sexual abuse of women and children. Other media stories parodied the issue of polygamy, describing products such as Polygamy Porter Beer, a local brew that has on its label the slogans "Why have just one" and "Bring some home to the wives." (Wasatch Brewery, Salt Lake City, Utah) As a result of the Olympics, issues like these were picked up by international media and brought to the attention and growing interest of a world audience.

The media's fascination with polygamy during the Olympics might have led to the erroneous impression that polygamy is exclusive to Mormonism and Utah. In fact, polygamy is practiced in other states and countries around the world. For some, polygamy is all about sex and the abuse of women and children, a horror operating under the guise of religion and a tradition that has to be stopped. For others, it is an expression of a strongly held religious belief and a practice that should be legal or at least decriminalized.

Former Canadian Prime Minister Pierre Elliot Trudeau has said, "The state has no business in the bedrooms of the nation." Did he mean the state and society should not scrutinize the private sexual lives of adults? The general consensus is that Trudeau meant that laws controlling consensual sex should be kept to a minimum. In the United States, polygamy is illegal and has been since the 1800s. There are some who believe that the state should apply the law and arrest those practicing polygamy. The feasibility of such an undertaking is daunting. According to some estimates 50,000 - 100,000 Americans practice polygamy. If all the adults were arrested, what would happen to their children? Should they be placed in state institutions or foster homes? And if so, would they be better off there? What resources would be needed to carry out this plan of action? Even if this undertaking were feasible, what would be the goal and result of such an intervention? Would the practice of polygamy be stopped? Would women and children be liberated?

Most polygamists consider themselves to be "True Mormons," and living polygamy is seen as a basic tenet of their faith and a practice that goes back generations. Rudger Clawson, the first person to be tried for polygamy, said, "I very much regret that the laws of my country should come in conflict with the laws of God, but whenever they do I shall invariably choose the latter." (Rudger Clawson, *Deseret News*, 3 Nov. 1884, Richard S. Van Wagoner, *Mormon Polygamy: A History*, Signature Books, 1989, p. 120) Indeed, present day believers still view the conflict as one of God's law versus man's law, and the choice for them is similar to Clawson's.

If legal action is taken to stop the practice of polygamy, it would probably reinforce practitioners' need for secrecy and for separation from non-believers and perpetuate their fear of persecution and prosecution.

In an extreme scenario, any intervention could provoke a violent reaction either internally (towards its own members) or externally (to those perceived as enemies). If intervening presents such serious problems, does this imply the law should not be enforced?

Some suggest that decriminalization or repealing the law is the route to take since it would not be possible to eliminate the practice. Does this mean that polygamy should be legalized because we can't stop it? But then, what about the abuse and exploitation? Because there may be considerable pitfalls to intervening or repealing existing laws, does this mean that the status quo is the appropriate position?

The debate over what to do about the practice of polygamy will not be quickly resolved. The issues surrounding it are complex, and decisions that will affect the lives of tens of thousands of people require serious thought. However, we cannot ignore the suffering that women and children face as documented by the growing number of accounts of abuse by former members of polygamous groups.

Owen Allred, head of the Apostolic United Brethren polygamist group, had this to say about child abuse in polygamist circles, "The thing is a stinking mess." (*New York Times*, Feb. 23, 2002)

For those who are aware of this "mess," and especially for those who are not, this book, *God's Brothel*, dealing with the problematic side of polygamy, provides an eye-opening look into the lives of the victims. The author, Andrea Moore-Emmett, is well-situated to tackle this complex issue. She was raised in the Mormon Church and has researched, given speeches around the country and written about polygamy for the past nine years. She has had the unique opportunity of meeting former members of polygamist groups and their families, as well as present-day members and leaders of these groups. Moore-Emmett has chosen to approach this subject by giving voice to 18 women. These women have varied experiences in a range of different polygamist groups and families, but they all share a common thread—deep pain and suffering as a result of the abuses that they have endured.

Although these women come from different backgrounds (Mormon and non-Mormon, polygamist and non-polygamist), they all shared the desire to become better people and live pure and spiritual lives. We follow them along their spiritual paths as their dreams of utopia become a life of pain and suffering. Through their experiences we learn that when power and control are exclusively in the hands of an authority, the only way to survive is subjugation of the self.

Each chapter is focused on one woman and devoted to her individual experiences, including the sexual and physical abuse that she and her children suffered, economic fraud, edicts against medical treatment, lack of education, incest, underage marriages and birth defects. It is hard to reconcile the image of women saying they are happy in polygamy with the riveting stories recounted in this book.

The fact remains that there are women who profess happiness in polygamous relationships. This should not, however, discount the reality of many others who live with deep physical, emotional and psychological scars. This book is a powerful testament to the abuses these 18 women have suffered and their tremendous courage in sharing their stories. Jan Shipps, the preeminent historian on the Mormon Church, noted, "[N]ow that these plural relationships once sanctified by the church have been tied to the victimization of women and children and possible abuse of government resources, continuing tolerance of the practice in the Mormon culture region will probably be less acceptable than it has been in the past half-century." (Jan Shipps, *Sojourner in the Promised Land: Forty Years Among the Mormons*, University of Illinois Press, 2000, p. 112-113)

What then should be done to protect these women and children? First, there is a need to acknowledge that these abuses occur. Next, there is a need to develop a coordinated response by child protection agencies, community groups, state and federal institutions and the Mormon Church. Andrea Moore-Emmett's book will provide further impetus to making the abuses associated with polygamy not just less acceptable but eventually, unacceptable.

Michael Kropveld
Executive Director, Info-Cult (Resource Centre on Cultic Thinking)
Montréal, Canada

INTRODUCTION

Unlike most people born into families that have been Mormon for several generations, I am not a descendent of polygamists. That omission in our pioneer family ancestry always caused my mother great regret since, according to her, it meant fewer blessings bestowed on all succeeding posterity. And, although I didn't grow up in Utah where polygamists are commonplace, polygamy was always a part of my life as a young Mormon girl. Polygamy loomed over my eternal future as a reverse "happily ever after." Even though I didn't embrace it any more than my maternal great-great-grandfather did, I knew it was just a matter of time before I would be expected to share my husband; if not in this life, then in the hereafter.

While attending my first two years of college at Ricks College, a Mormon Church-owned school in Idaho, I was up late one night indulging in a chocolate binge with my roommates. The nocturnal discussion turned to polygamy, and two of the girls started crying about their future prospects. They couldn't imagine how they were ever going to share a husband with other women. Another roommate assured us all that we would have a better understanding and acceptance of that commandment (*Doctrines and Covenants* Section 132) when we were more refined in our faith. My reaction on the subject was what it had always been as a girl, "I'll go to hell first."

Eventually, I left the Mormon faith but settled in Utah; and, in September 1996, I wrote a story that was published in *Salt Lake City Weekly*, one of Utah's alternative newspapers, about a young mother who, just three months before, had escaped from polygamy with her six children. It was the story of Vicky Prunty, and it is included in this book. When I interviewed Vicky, she confided to me that one of her goals was to create an organization to help other women who may wish to leave polygamy.

From experience, she clearly understood the unique difficulties of doing so and didn't want others to have to endure it alone.

Not long after that article appeared, former polygamist wife Rowenna Erickson contacted me wanting to be introduced to Prunty. They became close friends with a common cause; and, in March 1998, the two women, Rowenna's daughter, Stacy, and another former polygamist wife, Lillian Bowles, came together to form Tapestry of Polygamy, later changed to Tapestry Against Polygamy. They were guided by and given office space from another local women's organization: Justice, Economic Dignity and Independence for Women (JEDI). With JEDI's help, the Tapestry women were able to become non-profit and learn how to navigate in Utah's political maze. Several other former polygamist women considered helping Tapestry in its beginning, but decided to pursue other interests; still others volunteered later on and then left to work on their own anti-polygamist projects. (Information on Tapestry can be found at www.polygamy.org)

The women chose the word tapestry as a way to describe the interweaving of their individual stories with the common threads of their collective past. Their intent has always been as Prunty first articulated in 1996: To create a place where others wishing to flee from polygamy could come for help and aid in making the enormous transition. Other goals the women adopted were to educate an apathetic, uninformed public, and to lobby officials to adopt new laws to protect children and to enforce existing laws against polygamy and the abuses within the lifestyle.

The timing of their organization was prescient; two months later, Tapestry was thrown into an arena of worldwide media attention. International news services had quickly picked up a Utah story of the horrific beating of 16-year-old Mary Ann Kingston by her father, John Daniel Kingston, for running away from a forced marriage as the 15th wife of her 32-year-old uncle, David O. Kingston. Mary Ann was a minor and was taken into state protection with her identity and privacy closely guarded. The media turned to Tapestry for firsthand information concerning life in the extremely closed polygamous communities and to give Mary Ann a voice. That exposure gave Tapestry, among other things, the opportunity to effectively announce their services to many others who were looking for help in escaping polygamy.

This book is the result of their continuing work. It is an anthology of personal stories of the Tapestry members themselves and other women who wanted to share their stories. Each story is one more thread in the tapestry that is constantly being woven, revealing abuses endemic in the religiously-coerced polygamous lifestyle. Many more individuals were interviewed but could not be included in this book, mainly due to space constraints or because they wanted to keep their anonymity. All those whose stories are included have given permission to have their true names used; in certain cases, however, and by their request, names of other individuals have been changed.

Since these religious groups use a special language as a tool to separate members from outsiders, it may be of use for the reader to consult the glossary first and then refer to it throughout the reading of this book.

The blood atonement beliefs [that one must pay for one's sin with death] held by many Mormon fundamentalist polygamists force some who escape to live in hiding for fear of death. Many are without any family support and have lost their entire community and, in some cases, all that they have ever known and experienced in life. They usually have little or no education, having been mostly home-schooled or church-schooled and/or pulled out of their education at an early age to prepare for motherhood. They often have no job skills and no resources. Some of them have no birth certificate, no social security number and no driver's licenses. Many have lost their children to the group or to the fathers in court battles or simply through their struggle to leave, adding more loss.

Within polygamy, also referred to as Patriarchal Marriage by the early Mormon Church, women are the commodity and the exchange rate, forever in competition with one another, vying for the scarce resources and attentions of their lord and master who reigns supreme over them. In polygamy, children are mere extensions of their mothers and normally are their fathers' property. With so many children, they are thought of by fathers as a group rather than as individuals. Men, who believe they are the God of the home and who already live outside of societal norms, often make their children victims of ever more deviant and unimaginable abuses. Polygamy is patriarchy spun off into its furthest possible extreme.

Through the years in which I have interviewed hundreds of individuals, male and female, adults and children, from those who left the fundamentalist polygamist religions to those still deeply entrenched in them, I have wondered what it is that enables certain individuals to break free of the totalitarian beliefs while others remain clinging to a blind authoritarian faith.

One explanation is described by City University of New York Professor of Psychology and Psychiatry Robert Jay Lifton. Lifton calls the ability to evolve for personal transformation the "protean self" after Proteus, the Greek sea god of many forms. He sees a tendency toward a more open and flexible self that, rather than subscribing to either/or totalism, is many-sided in the quest for an ethical core. According to Lifton, the protean self avoids absolutes and holds out for the possibility of transformation and change. (Margaret Thaler Singer, foreword by Robert Jay Lifton, *Cults In Our Midst*, Jossey-Bass Inc. 1995, pp. XI - XIII)

From my own observations, the protean self, as manifested in women escaping polygamy, also has the ability to make great leaps across unknown chasms. Not a leap "of faith," but rather a leap "from faith" —to freedom of conscience and reason. It is with great responsibility that I put words to paper in the telling of the lives of such persons as these.

Though the exact definition of polygamy is the practice of having more than one spouse, indicating either gender, polygamy is most often associated with and used to refer to the marriage of more than one woman by one man or, more accurately, polygyny. In this country, those who have practiced this lifestyle historically, as well as those who practice it today, have referred to themselves as polygamists. Therefore, I will use *polygamy* rather than *polygyny* throughout this book.

I acknowledge that individuals often contract verbally with one another for and within a variety of sexual encounters and living arrangements. It is not the intent of this book to discuss these situations nor do I advocate for a government that peeks into the bedrooms of its citizens. My intent is to concentrate on polygamy dictated within a biblical-based context used to control women and children, usually originating with the Mormon Church and continuing into the present by Mormon fundamentalist polygamists and, more recently, by Christian polygamist groups and individuals.

Andrea Moore-Emmett

Salt Lake City, 2004

PART I: Contemporary Fundamentalist Polygamy in America

[I]f any man espouse a virgin, and desire to espouse another, and the first give her consent, and if he espouse the second, and they are virgins, and have vowed to no other man, then is he justified; he cannot commit adultery for they are given unto him; for he cannot commit adultery with that that belongeth unto him and to no one else.

And if he have ten virgins given unto him by this law, he cannot commit adultery, for they belong to him, and they are given unto him; therefore is he justified.

But if one or either of the ten virgins, after she is espoused, shall be with another man, she has committed adultery, and shall be destroyed....
　　　—Joseph Smith, *Doctrine and Covenants*, 132:61-63

And I command mine handmaid, Emma Smith, to abide and cleave unto my servant Joseph, and to none else. But if she will not abide this commandment she shall be destroyed, saith the Lord; for I am the Lord thy God, and will destroy her if she abide not in my law.
　　　—Joseph Smith, *Doctrine and Covenants*, 132:54

The Underpinnings of Mormon Polygamy

To understand the complex and convoluted issue of Mormon fundamentalist and Christian polygamy in this country, it is essential to know something of the history of its beginnings in the Mormon Church. It is also important to understand the Utah political and social climate, keeping in mind the larger national context of religious tolerance. Together, these factors have combined to make it possible for polygamy not only to continue but to flourish and grow.

In July 1843, Mormon Church president, founder and self-proclaimed prophet Joseph Smith, then based in Navuoo, Illinois, revealed the doctrine of polygamy to a few select followers as the only way to attain the "fullness of exaltation" in the afterlife. Smith called it the most important doctrine ever revealed to man on earth and said that without obedience to that principle, no man can ever attain the fullness of exaltation in celestial glory. (Historical Record 6:226) Later, after "the Saints" had relocated to the relative isolation of Utah, the full revelation was revealed to the church membership and recorded in the *Doctrine and Covenants* (D&C), Section 132, making it scripture to Mormon faithful.

Members of the Mormon Church, or as it is formally known, The Church of Jesus Christ of Latter-day Saints (LDS), expanded the practice of polygamy after establishing themselves in the Utah Territory in 1847. During the administration of Abraham Lincoln, federal lawmakers drafted and passed several bills designed to legislate polygamy out of existence. Those bills included the Morrill Anti-Bigamy Act, the Cullom Bill and the Poland Law. In 1856, the Republican Party platform named polygamy and slavery "twin relics of barbarism" and pledged to abolish them. These laws prevented Utah from being granted statehood.

Believing that polygamy was protected under the constitutional right to freedom of religion, Mormon Church leaders appealed the polygamy conviction of Brigham Young's secretary, George Reynolds, to the U.S. Supreme Court. On January 6, 1879, Chief Justice Morrison Waite delivered the landmark decision *Reynolds v. United States* that upheld the federal law against polygamy, saying one can believe what one wishes but one cannot practice a belief if doing so violates a valid and established law of the land. (Richard S. Van Wagoner, *Mormon Polygamy, A History*, Signature Books, 1989, p. 110, hereinafter "Van Wagoner")

Mormon reaction to the decision was one of complete defiance. Acting church president John Taylor denounced Chief Justice Waite's opinion as "bosh" in an 1879 *New York Times* interview. From the pulpit, Taylor said, "Polygamy is a divine institution. It has been handed down from God. I defy the United States. I will obey God." (*Salt Lake Tribune*, Jan. 6, 1880, Van Wagoner, 1989, p. 110)

In 1887, Congress passed the Edmunds Tucker Act, resulting in a major crusade against polygamists in the form of raids (then called "cohab hunts") and arrests. Those who would not comply with giving up plural wives and children served jail time or hid themselves through the Mormon underground. Others chose to move to Mormon colonies in Mexico and Canada. (Even today it is not uncommon in Utah to encounter Mormons born in Mexico who are not of Mexican descent but are from the still-thriving polygamist communities across the border.)

Still defiant, in 1885, George Q. Cannon, counselor of the Mormon First Presidency, proclaimed, "To comply with the request of our enemies, would be to give up all hope of ever entering into the glory of God, the Father, and Jesus Christ, the son. So intently interwoven is this precious doctrine with the exaltation of men and women in the great hereafter that it cannot be given up without giving up at the same time all hope of immortal glory." (*Juvenile Instructor* 20:136, May 1, 1885)

But in 1890, Mormon Church President Wilford Woodruff issued a proclamation now known as the Manifesto, pledging to Congress that Mormons had given up polygamy, thus paving the way for statehood. The Manifesto was printed in the *Doctrines and Covenants* as an official declaration, rather than scripture, while Section 132 continues to stand as scripture in the Mormon Church to this day, providing some with justification for polygamy.

In truth, Mormons, including Woodruff, continued to marry plural wives until church president Joseph Fielding Smith was forced to issue a second Manifesto in 1904. That Manifesto also never became scripture, but church members were excommunicated for practicing polygamy.

Mormons who could never accept the Manifesto and betray their plural families believed the leaders were plunging the church into apostasy. These individuals split from the mainstream Mormon Church, claiming a new line of authority, which they traced to President John Taylor through John Woolley. John Taylor's son, John W. Taylor, maintained that in 1886, while living on the underground at John Woolley's home, his father inquired of the Lord if it would not be right under the circumstances to discontinue polygamy. John claimed that in his father's papers he found a document recording the response: "[T]he Lord told (my father) that the principle of plural marriage would never be overcome." At his excommunication trial before the Quorum of the Twelve Apostles, young Taylor later said that several individuals, including Joseph F. Smith, took the document and made a copy of it. (Van Wagoner, 1989, pp. 182-183) In 1933, the Taylor family donated the original handwritten 1886 revelation to the Mormon Church, which has never tested it for authenticity nor released it to the public.

Mormon fundamentalist polygamists maintain that President John Taylor secretly ordained several priesthood holders (including John Woolley) to continue the practice of polygamy through a special dispensation of priesthood authority. They further believe that Taylor gave the priesthood holders the authority both to perform polygamous marriages and to ordain others with authority to perform polygamous marriages to ensure that children would be born to polygamous parents each year thereafter until Christ's second coming at the millennium. (Ibid.)

Some Mormon Church members, historians, apologists and fundamentalist Mormons are prone to nostalgically romanticize that Mormon women were happy polygamist wives. Some, in defense of polygamy, have gone so far as to assert that polygamy was an early feminist movement offering an alternative within marriage giving women freedom, security and an opportunity for self-development. (Utah NOW Conference, guest speaker, Elizabeth Joseph, 1997) However, the letters and diaries of the women in polygamy in the early years of the church suggest that they were not happy and that their seeking employment stemmed not from unusual flexibility and opportunities offered by polygamy, but from the poverty, self-martyrdom and unfulfilling marital unions that characterized polygamy.

Ellis R. Shipp, one of four wives, wrote of her unhappiness just three weeks before deciding her best avenue to self-fulfillment was to go to medical school. "Once I was happy for I thought I was beloved - Yes, I thought I knew I was - probably I was then - but Oh, it is past. I feel my heart breaking and I sigh over what has been, but now has ceased to be. [A]nd I felt that the realization of such an event would deprive me either of my life or reason." (Ellis Shipp Musser, comp. and ed., *The Early Autobiography and Diary of Ellis Reynolds Shipp, M.D.*, Salt Lake City:

Deseret News Press, 1962, p. 162, Marilyn Warenski, *Patriarchs and Politics*, McGraw-Hill, 1978, p. 159)

In researching his book on Joseph Smith's wives, Todd Compton found that husbands were unable to support their numerous women and children. "[W]e see another characteristic of polygamy: the men often were willing to add plural wives to their families, but after the marriage took place found they were unable to support the multiple families adequately." (Todd Compton, *In Sacred Loneliness, The Plural Wives of Joseph Smith*, Signature Books, Salt Lake City, 1998, p. 199)

When women complained, they were met with a rebuff rather than sympathy. On one occasion, Brigham Young called the membership together and, using his own wives as an example, gave the women of the church an ultimatum: "My wives have got to do one of two things, either round up their shoulders to endure the afflictions of this world and live the religion, or they may leave, for I will not have them about me." (Brigham Young, *Journal of Discourses*, 4:55. Marilyn Warenski, *Patriarchs and Politics*, McGraw-Hill, 1978, p. 161)

On another occasion, Young told the women of the Mormon Church, "You sisters may say that plural marriage is very hard for you to bear. It is no such thing. [I]f it is the duty of a husband to take a wife. It is the duty of the woman to submit cheerfully." (Young, *Journal of Discourses*, 17:159)

Contemporary Mormon and Christian-based Polygamy

Mormon and Christian fundamentalist polygamists are scattered throughout the United States, Mexico and Canada with most located in the Western areas. The majority of polygamists reside in Utah, nestled within its 72 percent Mormon population.

Since 1980, the number of polygamists in Utah, the surrounding Western states and other states has been estimated at approximately 30,000. Tapestry Against Polygamy estimates the number to be closer to 100,000, regardless of out-migration by disaffected members. Reasons for the vastly differing but clearly growing numbers are varied. First of all, most Mormon fundamentalist polygamist men admonish women of childbearing age to have one child per year and they strictly prohibit birth control. Second, since some polygamists do not file a birth certificate with the state when a child is born, it is impossible for the state to count these individuals. Third, the largest number of polygamists are found within the independents—those who live in Mormon polygamous families but are not affiliated with a group and often go uncounted in these official estimates. Some members of the mainstream Mormon Church are also closeted polygamists. These arrangements are so well protected that they are not even known to neighbors much less the state, which they fear will prosecute them, or the mainstream church, which would excommunicate them. These individuals are never accounted for in official estimates. Fourth, new groups continue to spring up among Mormons seeking a form of their religion without the changes to early principles. Some of these groups are unknown to authorities and they, as well as the older groups, consistently draw members from the mainstream Mormon Church. Another influx of polygamists resulted from a Christian minister, Steve Butt of the Broken Shackles Ministry, and his wives, who began a small but now growing following in Utah during the late 1990s.

Many smaller Mormon and Christian fundamentalist polygamist groups will often form and then, for various reasons, disintegrate after a short period of time. Some of the individuals of these groups convert to other established groups, become independent polygamists or abandon the practice altogether.

The main groups that have been in existence for at least five years are described below.

The Apostolic United Brethren (AUB) is centered in Bluffdale, Utah, but has settlements in Pinesdale, Montana, Pleasant Valley, Nevada, and Ozumba, Mexico, where they have built a temple. The AUB also has settlements in various parts of Utah including Rocky Ridge, Cedar City and Motoqua. The aging Owen Allred is the current leader with Lamoine Jensen next in line. There are an estimated 7,000 total members.

The Fundamentalist Church of Jesus Christ of Latter-day Saints (FLDS) is located in the twin cities of Hildale, Utah, and Colorado City, Arizona. They also have two settlements in British Columbia, Canada (in Bountiful and Creston), and one in Mexico, and have recently purchased land in Texas and Colorado. The Hildale/Colorado City group is led by Warren Jeffs. A schism of this group, known as the Second Ward, began a community known as Centennial Park just down the highway in Arizona. Johnny Timpson reigns over this group as their priesthood leader. FLDS membership is estimated at 10,000-15,000.

The True and Living Church of Jesus Christ of Saints of the Last Days (TLC) resides in the small Mormon town of Manti, Utah. It is led by Jim Harmston, who has restored two buildings in downtown Manti as a headquarters that replicates the early Mormon Church buildings of Nauvoo, Illinois. Harmston's followers average 300 in number.

The Church of the First Born of the Fullness of Times is headquartered at Colonia LeBaron in Chihuahua, Mexico with members in Texas, California and in Juab County, Utah. The current leader is Joel LeBaron. There are an estimated 500 current members.

The **Church of the Lamb of God** is led by Fred Collier with members in Hanna, Utah, and Mexico. In Hanna, Collier's members occupy an old Mormon meeting house where they operate a printing press and a winery. Membership fluctuates at around 100 members.

The **Latter-day Church of Christ** is now led by Paul Kingston and is a Salt Lake-based religion with members and multi-million dollar businesses in Utah, Idaho and Nevada. Though the church has grown wealthy off the backs of its members and immigrant labor (including Mexican immigrant mine workers who are paid a fraction of local prevailing wages for miners), members live in dire poverty, which is taught to be a virtue. Their doctrine of intermarriage began with the second leader of the group, John Ortell Kingston, who at the age of 30 married his niece, Coreen Gustafson and his half-sister, Kathleen Tucker. He later married two other nieces among a total of 13 wives. There are approximately 2,000 members of this religious clan.

The **Church of Jesus Christ of the United Order** is led by Luis Gonzales though, at this date, Gonzales is serving a prison term. Members reside in Sacramento, California, and in a community in Jackson County, Missouri, under the leadership of Floren LeBaron who defected from his family's Mormon fundamentalist polygamist group. There are an estimated 70 members of this group. (The original LeBaron group is believed to be disbanded with the exception of a colony in Mexico. Not only has the Mexico colony grown but they have also proliferated in Southern California and Utah as well.)

The **Righteous Branch** is located in Paiquin, Utah, with its own temple and is led by Gerald Peterson Jr. who, at this date, resides with his wives in Reno, Nevada. This clan is estimated to have about 100 members.

The Church of Jesus Christ is located in Jackson County, Missouri, and led by Roger Billings whose members have carved out an underground community awaiting the end of time and the return of Jesus Christ. Numbers for this secretive group are not available.

The Patriarchal Hierarchy is the continuing religion begun by Tom Green at Green Haven, a row of trailers on Utah's West Desert. Green is now serving a prison sentence but continues to maintain a semblance of control with his scattered members, estimated to number 50, living in Utah, Nevada and Southern California.

The Patriarchal Christian Fellowship of God's Free Men and Women is the most organized of the Christian fundamentalist polygamists. Begun by Steve Butt out of his self-styled Broken Shackles Ministry, Butt's following is connected through the Internet all over the United States. He and his wives moved from Maine to Utah, then to Washington state, and were last known to be in Texas. Butt has said that he counts around 14,000 members in the United States.

Other Mormon fundamentalist polygamists from different groups and some independents have moved to Jackson County, Missouri, since the tragedy of September 11, seeing it as a sign of the end of times. They meet with a common alternating bishop while maintaining their separate identities or group affiliations. This is an ever-fluctuating, loose group whose numbers are impossible to estimate.

Independent Mormon and Christian fundamentalist polygamists and some extended family groups make up the largest numbers of polygamists and are led by the patriarch of each of their families. They are spread throughout the United States and any estimate of their numbers would be only a far-reaching guess.

While the Mormon Church itself no longer condones polygamy and continues to excommunicate members who are discovered to be living the practice, the attitude between Mormons and Mormon fundamentalist polygamists is that of kissing cousins with more similarities than differences. A certain amount of deference is shown to one another, while at the same time each side condemns the other as apostate, claiming it is acting without proper authority. They share the same religious genesis with Joseph Smith as the prophet and founder of the restored gospel on earth, as well as a belief in, and veneration for, other early Mormon leaders. They sing the same Mormon hymns, pray in the same manner and share the same scriptures, which include the *Book of Mormon, Pearl of Great Price, Doctrine and Covenants*, and the Bible.

Mormons are, on the one hand, proud of their polygamist ancestry and, on the other, embarrassed about how that history reflects on the modern church, which has attempted to move toward an appearance of being mainstream Christian. This has caused great consternation from the Evangelical Christian community, which (along with other Protestant religions) does not consider the Mormon Church to be a Christian religion. (The New Mormon Challenge, Christian Apologetics, Biola University, La Mirada, CA, Conference 2003) Still, Mormons believe polygamy will be restored at another time to be lived again and most certainly will be lived in the afterlife. With the commandment to live polygamy canonized as scripture to all believing Mormons, it is impossible for them to outright repudiate it.

As Mormons struggle with this uncomfortable paradox, the embarrassment translates into an interesting history re-write. Even when pressed, some tour guides at Brigham Young's historical home in Salt Lake City refuse to tell tourists that the numerous bedrooms of the home housed many of his 56 wives. In his 552-page biography of Brigham

Young, Mormon historian Preston Nibley never mentions that Young had more than one wife. And, in an unprecedented appearance on the Larry King Show in September 1998, Mormon Church President Gordon Hinckley told King that the church has no doctrine that supports polygamy. After the broadcast, I contacted Mormon Church spokesman Dale Bills. He informed me that Hinckley was referring to polygamy as it is lived today and that *Doctrine and Covenants* Section 132, "[S]tands as is without added scripture to negate, modify or change it in any way."

The Mormon Church also practices what has been called ecclesiastical polygamy—the practice of marrying one man to several women in Mormon temples for eternity. Thus, if a man marries a woman and she dies or they get a civil divorce, he is still considered "sealed" (married for eternity; see glossary) to her and can remarry and be sealed to a second, third or more women so long as he is civilly married to only one woman at a time. Women, however can be sealed to only one man, as they are not allowed multiple husbands on earth or in the afterlife.

Prosecution of Polygamy

As what could be described as a theocracy, Utah has precious little separation of church and state. Utah citizens, with their heavily Mormon majority, have voted into office Mormon governors for most of the state's history. The state legislature remains consistently near 90 percent Mormon, and the congressional delegation has been 100 percent Mormon for decades. Further, several polygamist men serve in local government positions including as mayors, Utah State Housing Development Advisory Councilmen and city councilmen.

Although Utah has a statute against polygamy as well as a state constitution that specifically dictates that polygamy shall be forever prohibited, making it a felony, the Utah Attorney General's Office said in 1999 that it is not a crime to live in polygamy. In 1998, Utah Governor Mike Leavitt said he thought polygamy was a protected freedom, only to later retract his statement after being informed that it is against the law. With continuing official winks and other dynamics at play in Utah, polygamists have proliferated throughout the state, enjoying a visible presence with repercussions only occurring when Tapestry Against Polygamy and other anti-polygamy activists have prodded officials or when polygamists break the unspoken rule of staying to themselves, nearly forcing officials to prosecute them. As some of the less paranoid polygamists often say, "That prosecution dog don't hunt."

Successfully prosecuting cases arising from polygamy requires that law enforcement, investigators and prosecutors understand the unique dynamics of polygamous families and groups. As Sarah's story in Chapter 18 of this book demonstrates, prosecuting these cases as garden-variety domestic cases may place the victims in grave danger. A learning curve is involved in understanding the dynamics of these relationships and the vulnerabilities they give rise to.

When prosecution does occur in Utah, it is usually when polygamists have engaged in visible, violent crimes or when they parade their wives to the media, proudly flouting the law. The LeBaron's blood atoning killing spree in the 1970s (described in Chapter 8) and the Lafferty's blood atonement murders in 1984 brought polygamy into public view. Also capturing the media's attention was the killing of polygamist John Singer in 1979 and a retaliatory bombing of a Mormon Church in 1988 by Singer's family members and the Swapp brothers. The bombing led the FBI to Utah for a thirteen-day standoff that ended with the death of police officer Fred House.

In 1982, Murray, Utah, Police Officer Royston Potter was fired from his job for failure to comply with his oath to uphold laws, including laws against polygamy. Still, Utah continues to employ numerous polygamists as policemen.

In 1991, The Zion Society of Ogden, Utah, led by Arvin Shreeve, was raided by authorities. Shreeve was convicted of sodomy and sent to prison for having sex with underage boys. Several of his 25 wives served jail sentences or were put on probation and on the Utah sex offender list for using underage girls to model their home-sewn line of lingerie.

In 1998, Utah became a worldwide stage for the sensational child abuse trial of Daniel Kingston for beating his 16-year-old daughter who was trying to escape a forced marriage as the 15th wife of her 32-year-old uncle David Kingston and the incest trial of the uncle. In each case, polygamy was either not allowed to be mentioned or was peripheral to other crimes alleged. Avoiding 15 years for second-degree felony child abuse, Daniel entered a no-contest plea to a reduced charge of a third-degree felony. He was given 28 weeks in a county jail and a $2,700 fine at his April 1999 sentencing. That same year, David was convicted of one count of incest and one count of unlawful sexual conduct with a minor, both third degree felonies. He was sentenced to two consecutive 0-5 year prison terms but served only four years of a 10-year sentence. He was released in June 2003.

In late 2000, the Utah Attorney General's Office hired an investigator, Ron Barton, to investigate polygamy. Soon after his appointment, however, Barton, an LDS Church member, told me it was his personal feeling that polygamy should be given religious freedom status. Nearly a year later, I spoke with him again. He was still somewhat ambivalent but, after struggling with his words, he finally admitted that the lifestyle seemed to breed abuses and, in light of that, polygamy should be kept illegal. Since taking office in January, 2001, Attorney General Mark

Shurtleff has vowed to crack down on abuses within polygamy, but only where there is ample evidence.

One case with ample evidence was that of Tom Green. Barton and Utah's Juab County prosecutor, David Leavitt, finally brought independent polygamist Tom Green to trial. He was charged with bigamy and criminal non-support after Green goaded authorities on national television with his flagrant disregard for the law. The latter charge stemmed from bilking taxpayers out of more than $150,000 in welfare benefits. Green's justification was pulled from his anti-government rhetoric of "bleeding the beast" to benefit God's chosen and to help bring down the government, a common theme in most polygamist groups. He was found guilty on both charges on May 18, 2001 and was sentenced to five years in prison on August 23, 2001. Additionally, on August 28, 2002, Green was sentenced to the minimum sentence of five years to life in prison for the first degree felony conviction of child rape due to impregnating one of his wives when she was 13 (others say they married when she was only nine). He was never charged with incest, although he married two of his stepdaughters. (It should be noted that prosecutor David Leavitt was defeated in the next election.)

International awareness about polygamy increased following the June 5, 2002 abduction of 14-year-old Elizabeth Smart from her Salt Lake City bedroom. Nine months later, on March 12, 2003, she was discovered on the streets of nearby Sandy, Utah, with Brian David Mitchell and his wife, Wanda Barzee. Mitchell explained that he had taken Smart in response to a revelation from God telling him she was the first of seven polygamous wives that were to be given to him. Mitchell and Barzee were taken into custody and Elizabeth was returned to her family, with the incident attracting embarrassing international attention for Utah once more.

On July 24, 2003, Jeremy Kingston was arrested for one count of incest for his marriage to his 15-year-old cousin, who is also his aunt; the marriage had produced two daughters. In January 2004, Jeremy was sentenced to one year in jail and three years of probation.

On August 6, 2003, police officer Rodney Holm was ordered to stand trial on bigamy and sex charges for wedding his 16-year-old sister-in-law. Holm was offered a plea deal but refused through his attorney who called the charges religious persecution. Holm was convicted of a single bigamy count and two sex charges.

And coming full circle, on August 1, 2003, Mary Ann Kingston, the girl who was beaten by her father for running away from the marriage to her uncle, filed a multi-million dollar class action suit against the polygamist Latter-day Church of Christ and their businesses for punitive damages, pain and suffering and imprisonment.

Other states also have prosecuted polygamists for incest and abuse. From 2001 through 2004, prosecutors in Sacramento, California, tried and convicted two Mormon men who, separately and secretly led their own inner polygamist groups, the Church of Jesus Christ of the United Order and the Universal Church of Jesus Christ. In July 2002, Luis Gonzales was convicted of 20 counts of child molestation, one count of spousal abuse and one count of bigamy. He was sentenced to 50 years in prison. Allen Rex Harrod was charged with 97 counts of molestation, and one of his wives, Irene Hunt, was accused of complicity. In February of 2004, Allen received a life sentence and Irene was ordered to serve 15 years.

Of Minnesota's 42,000 Laotian Hmong immigrants, whose traditional culture includes polygamy, 7,600 currently live in polygamy. (AsianWeek, 11-22-2002) Hmong women have murdered, stabbed and shot their husbands who bring home young wives.

A court in Pennsylvania, in connection with a custody case, banned Mormon fundamentalist Stanley Shepp from discussing plural marriage with his minor daughter. He appealed, and in May, 2004, the Pennsylvania Supreme Court heard arguments in the case.

Fresno, California, saw the worst murder in its history in March 2004, with nine family members shot to death and stacked in a pile. The media reported Marcus Wesson calmly walking out of his house covered in blood. Wesson and his followers lived polygamy and incest as part of his self-styled, Bible-based religion. One of Wesson's victims was his daughter, who was also the mother of his child.

In April of 2004, the story of a 21-year-old Arizona girl from Maricopa County came to the attention of Arizona officials. At the age of 11, the girl had been forced into a polygamous relationship with her stepfather. The mother and stepfather, Stanley and Janice Rimer, also had another woman involved as a plural wife at the time.

Other cases continue to develop, catching officials off guard and promising more embarrassment for Utah and other states.

Religious Freedom or Freedom to Exploit?

In 1999, the Utah chapter of the American Civil Liberties Union (ACLU) responded to the polygamy issue by reiterating the 1991 national ACLU statement which reads, "The ACLU believes that criminal and civil laws prohibiting or penalizing the practice of plural marriage violate constitutional protections of freedom of expression and association, freedom of religion and privacy for personal relationships among consenting adults." (ACLU Board Minutes, Policy #91, April 1991)

It is my opinion that in taking this stand, the ACLU chose to ignore the civil and human rights violations against thousands of women and children involved in polygamy. This brings into question how well the

U.S. Constitution is interpreted in regards to the First and Fourteenth Amendments. While the U.S. was founded on basic freedoms, including the freedom of religion, there is a distinction between belief and conduct. One can believe whatever one wishes; however, one cannot practice a belief if such practice violates a valid law. Since *Reynolds*, that distinction has continued to be upheld by the United States Supreme Court. Further, the ACLU position runs counter to the United Nations Convention on the Elimination of Discrimination Against Women, which was signed by 162 countries.

Extending the religious freedom argument further, little difference exists between Afghanistan's once powerful Taliban's extreme religious beliefs with its oppressive and dangerous effects on women and those of the Mormon fundamentalist polygamist and Christian polygamists, other than the fact that the latter live in America. The denial of education to females, shaming the female form into hiding under extreme covering clothing and arranged marriages are just some of the many similarities. Still, many individuals continue to dismiss these American oppressors merely as individuals following their religious beliefs and personal choices.

In 1999, the National Organization for Women (NOW) passed a resolution supporting Tapestry Against Polygamy, condemning the abuses in polygamy and awarding Tapestry leaders with NOW's prestigious Courageous Woman of the Year Award. But in a wide departure from their parent organization, the Utah NOW chapter defended the right of polygamist wives who choose to live that lifestyle, "[women] should be able to decide how they want to live as consenting adults." (Utah NOW newsletter, August 1999). The local NOW chapter expressed uneasiness that Utah bigamy laws, which polygamists can be charged with, could also affect same sex couples. (Ibid.)

The local NOW position at that time seemed to imply that they condone any conditions and acts to be done to a woman as long as that woman is consenting. By that standard, one could argue the same in regards to the phenomenon of battered women who remain with or return to their abusive partners.

The comparison to same sex couples remains a bizarre juxtaposition. Polygamy is about one powerful man collecting a submissive harem of women as property and a herd of children with no individual identity. Homosexuality is about the sexual orientation of two committed equal partners asking for the same rights and recognition for their union as are given to equal partnered heterosexual couples. Further, in contrast to homosexual couples who contribute to society, most polygamists rely on food stamps, Medicaid, economic development funds and other government services to support their increasingly large families. Between July 2002 and July 2003, families belonging to the Fundamentalist Church of Latter-day Saints (FLDS) living in Hildale, Utah, and Colorado City, Arizona, received more than $3 million in food stamps and cash assistance. ("Time To Close The Circle," *Salt Lake Tribune*, 3-15-04, citing Utah Dept. of Health) Polygamists proudly call their dependence on government programs "bleeding the beast" and seek government assistance as an intentional effort to bring down the U.S. Government—ironically, the same government they expect to protect their desires to have sex with young girls and relatives under the freedom of religion part of the First Amendment.

In 2002, the Utah NOW chapter changed leadership and did an about face of its policy in regards to polygamy. The local chapter is no longer at odds with national NOW policy and works closely with Tapestry in their efforts. During November 2003, I became the Utah NOW president, making polygamy a priority issue.

Polygamy Beyond Utah and Mormons

Although this book does not deal with polygamist cultures in other countries or those who have migrated to the United States, such as the Hmong of Laos or members of Muslim communities, they are mentioned here for perspective in the larger polygamist world community.

A large majority—980 of the 1,154 past or present societies for which anthropologists have data—have allowed a man to have more than one wife. Six of these societies are also polyandrous, meaning women having multiple spouses. (Robert Wright, *The Moral Animal*, Vintage Books, 1994, pp. 90 and 401; numbers from computerized data-base derived from G. P. Murdock's *Ethnographic Atlas*, gathered courtesy of Steven J. C. Gaulin) For a variety of reasons, including politics and preserving family ownership of property, more than 65 percent of today's world populations belong to a community that allows polygamy, including Nigeria, much of the Middle East, Laos, the Russian Republic of Ingushetia, Nepal, India and the Yanomamo of the Amazon. In all of these communities, women are already otherwise discriminated against, and only very few individuals within these populations ever attempt to practice polygamy. Perhaps the reason for its lack of popularity is best illustrated by polygamous societies in the Middle East, where plural wives refer to one another as "troubles," and in Afghanistan where girls have been known to set themselves on fire rather than to marry into such unions.

In one extreme, polygamy practiced by the Yanomamo people of the Amazon consists of the men of one village sneaking up on and attacking and killing the men of a neighboring village. They grab the screaming babies, bash their brains out on the rocks and spear the older children, pinning their bodies to the ground, or throw them off the cliffs.

The children's death sentence stems from their paternity. In triumph, the Yanomamo men then lead the captured women back to their new lives as secondary wives. (Howard Bloom, *The Lucifer Principle, A Scientific Expedition Into The Forces Of History*, The Atlantic Monthly Press, 1995, pp. 37-38)

In 1997, the Campaign Against Polygamy and Women Oppression in Africa and Worldwide (CAPWONA) was formed in Nigeria. The directors of the agency maintain that their research shows that polygamy is unequivocally the major factor responsible for poverty, corruption, illiteracy and diseases that constitute the galling gap between the Western and African societies. (Personal e-mail from Talwo Onalaja, Chief Co-ordinator, CAPWONA, 10-6-01)

Although it is tempting to point to other cultures where polygamy exists to legitimize Mormon fundamentalist and Christian polygamy as a natural male inclination, there are significant problems in doing so. While the greed of genes may be a driving primordial force, conditions and certain acts toward women and children in one culture or country do not necessarily constitute a definer of standards for all other nations, particularly from an undeveloped culture, as the Yanomamo illustrate.

Much is said about many women in polygamy being consenting adults who willingly choose to live as plural wives and who are very happy. There can be no consent when girls are born into polygamy and, through isolation and limited education, do not know of any other choices. There can be no consent when women are recruited and go through the conversion process without understanding how mind-control takes place physically and mentally.

Polygamy can be seen as one of the many ways women historically have been persuaded by patriarchy to participate in their own oppression and collusion against themselves and one another. Such complicity, however, does not equate to a reasoned choice any more than it did for that certain segment of African slaves in America who fought against their own emancipation.

Continuing the so-called consenting adults line of thinking further, female genital mutilation has been performed as far back as 502 CE, as women themselves, who have suffered and witnessed death resulting from its practice, continue to line up their own daughters to have the mutilation repeated. It has thus been a practice that is perpetrated against women by women so that men can be assured of receiving a virgin bride. (Marilyn French, *The War Against Women*, Summit Books, 1992, pp. 106-114)

For more than 1,000 years, millions of mothers in China suffering with continuously painful, crippled and mutilated feet, forced their daughters to endure the same horrors through the practice of foot binding in the name of male erotica. (Andrea Dworkin, *Woman Hating*, E. P. Dutton, 1974, pp. 95-117)

In the United States's recent past, countless women fought against suffrage—women who believed the patriarchal propaganda of the times that said they and their own mothers, sisters and daughters were unable to carry out the responsibility of voting for their own government.

While happiness can be a very subjective state of mind or ruthlessly obtained at the expense of another's misery, women have confided to me during interviews that they were commanded by their leaders to be happy and admonished that happiness was their duty. Some were told that if they were not happy it was because they allowed Satan into their lives. I observed that women said they were happy and became very adept at the appearance of happiness during their time in polygamy to avoid the judgment of others within the group or to defend to outsiders the lifestyle to which they had committed themselves. In every case in which some of these same women later became free of polygamy, they confessed that while they were claiming happiness during their time inside of polygamy they were, in fact, miserable. One woman described having to leave polygamy because she felt she was dying from the inside out.

It is also important to address the biblical justification used to support polygamy since it is one of the reasons Joseph Smith gave for inquiring of the Lord on the matter and one that Mormon fundamentalist polygamists use today. And it is the Bible, of course, that is the basis for the Christian polygamists' beliefs.

Historical scholar Gerda Lerner writes that the biblical practice of taking concubines and plural wives grew out of Mesopotamian and Hebrew law rather than from religious tenet. Further, she maintains that evidence shows the practice was codified into those laws as it evolved either out of, or as a precursor to, slavery of those times. (Gerda Lerner, *The Creation of Patriarchy*, Oxford University Press, 1986, pp. 76-122)

According to theologian Uta Ranke-Heinemann, Jesus (whether one believes him to be divine or only historical) rejected the practice of taking additional wives and rebuked the disciples for their polygamist mindset as recorded in Matthew 19:2-12, and again in the Sermon on the Mount. (Uta Ranke-Heinemann, *Eunuchs for The Kingdom of Heaven*, Doubleday, 1990, pp. 33-36)

The Current Legal Maze

In 2003, a Utah couple identified as G. Lee Cook and D. Cook asked the Salt Lake County Clerk to issue them a marriage licence for a third person—a woman identified as J. Bronson. After being denied the licence, they hired Utah civil rights attorney Brian Barnard and sued, claiming that their constitutional right to free exercise of religion had been violated. (*Bronson v. Swenson*, No. 02:04-CV-0021 D. Utah 2004)

At the same time, Utah polygamist Tom Green began appealing his own convictions for bigamy citing the U.S. Supreme Court's June 2003 ruling in *Lawrence v. Texas*, which struck down a Texas law criminalizing sodomy. His appeal was rejected.

In *Lawrence*, the Court held that there is a federal constitutional right of privacy that prohibits the state from banning homosexual sex. Further, the Court in *Lawrence* cited an emerging awareness that liberty gives substantial protection to adult persons in deciding how to conduct their private lives in sexual matters.

Marci Hamilton, law professor and constitutional law scholar at Benjamin N. Cardozo School of Law, writes that "Lawrence was a broad, important decision. But it's important to remember that it was not a decision about the very public institution of marriage, but rather private, sexual acts." ("Is a Prohibition on Polygamy Constitutional?", Marci Hamilton, www.writ.news.findlaw.com/hamilton.20040212.html) Hamilton maintains that legal precedent firmly rejects free exercise challenges of religion to anti-polygamy laws, citing the Supreme Court's decision in 1879 in *Reynolds v. United States*, the early Mormon test case in which the Court rejected a challenge to the law holding that an individual's religious beliefs are no defense to the application of a general law to religious conduct.

Hamilton explains that the Supreme Court of Massachusetts recently drew on *Lawrence* in a case about marriage, but it emphasized equality, not privacy rights. In *Goodridge v. Department of Health*, the court held that under the Massachusetts Constitution, homosexual persons have an equal right to marriage and the benefits of marriage. Hamilton writes that the court was concerned that gay persons were being relegated to second-class citizen status because they lacked access to marriage. (Ibid.)

The conclusion of the Massachusetts court that two equal partners have a constitutional right to participate in marriage regardless of sexual orientation was based on grounds of equality. Would-be polygamists already have the right to marry a single other individual. Taking a third or more women into a union is changing the very nature of marriage and is the antithesis of equality due to the power imbalance inherent in polygamy, where one male wields power over several women, as demonstrated in the stories of the women in this book.

University of Calgary Political Science Professor Tom Flanagan observes that polygamous societies are highly unequal and a deadly foe of constitutional government, turning women into a form of private property. (T. Flanagan, "Democracy, Polygamy and the Sexual Constitution," *National Post*, 5-23-01) Naomi Schaefer, a Fellow at the Ethics and Public Policy Center, writes that polygamy is not an activity whose effects are restricted to the bedroom and consenting adults, as the plaintiffs in *Lawrence v. Texas* argued was the case with respect to sodomy. Rather, polygamy seems to corrupt civil society as a whole, destroying education, individual rights and the rule of law—in other words the foundations of democratic governance. Further, Schaefer compares polygamy to slavery, saying even a single instance can fundamentally alter a society. (Naomi Schaefer, *Los Angeles Times*, 2-13-04)

During America's shameful days of slavery, education was denied in order to maintain control, just as it is in America's polygamy today. Laura's story in this book tells of how she was pulled from the group's school at age thirteen to began preparing for motherhood. In Lillian's story, children receive inadequate education from the group's school. When one half of a population, females, are denied their fundamental right to an education, or where girls and boys are barely educated at all, society is most definitely altered from its full human, social and economic development.

Further, the male ownership of women and children affords the owner complete discretion to do with his dehumanized property as he sees fit. Polygamists live proudly outside the law, feeling themselves above man's law and justifying their acts, including illegal and devious acts, as being dictated by a higher authority.

As to the *Bronson v. Swenson* lawsuit in Utah, Schaefer notes that the harm to children within polygamy should be enough to insure that the suit does not succeed. She then goes on to site the 1944 Supreme Court ruling in *Prince vs. Massachusetts*. In that case, the Court concluded that parents are not free to make martyrs of their children. Schaefer concludes saying, "Unfortunately, in polygamous communities, one necessarily entails the other." (Ibid.)

Moreover, in *Lawrence* the Court held that adults may engage in private sexual conduct that does not involve coercion or injury. As seen in the stories of the women in this book, who escaped from 10 of the 11 long-standing polygamist groups and from several independent polygamist families, injury and coercion are the hallmarks of contemporary Bible-based fundamentalist polygamy.

The Lure of Polygamy and Other Fundamentalism

Naomi Schaefer asked, "What is it about polygamy that makes the roots so deep and destructive?" (Ibid.) Human beings are social creatures who form group attachments as a normal and necessary function for survival. We are also greatly influenced by, and respond to, dominance behavior and deference behavior. It is a chemical and emotional makeup that leaves us vulnerable to exploitation of group affiliations. (Wendy Ford, Harvard

University, "The Role of Emotions During Cult Conversions," 2-14-92)

After Elizabeth Smart was taken by Brian Mitchell and Wanda Barzee as a second wife, she was forced into dependency, making these two individuals her entire universe. Looking very much like Jesus, Mitchell preached fundamentalist Mormonism, which could not have been difficult for the young Mormon girl to feel comfortable with. Though she was underage, her gullibility and compliance would not have been any less had she been 18 or older when she was kidnapped or had she turned 18 during her ordeal.

Many polygamists find that recruiting Mormon women into polygamy is very easy, as shown in the stories of Tammy, Janice and even college-educated Vicky and Cindy in this book. Mormon fundamentalist polygamists are adept at using the Mormon scriptures, mainly *Doctrine and Covenants* Section 132, as a persuasive, cautionary tale to believing Mormon women and girls. Emma, Joseph Smith's first wife, according to the scripture, is told by God that she will be destroyed if she does not accept polygamy.

With the power of the scriptures, polygamy continues its enslavement of women who are manipulated into believing that to do otherwise is to reap eternal damnation; by believing, however, they make of their lives a hell on earth.

It is often difficult for educated, economically stable people with control over their own lives (especially those who make decisions in their lives free from the dictates of a religion) to understand why women enter or fail to leave polygamy. The women who have willingly joined these groups, as well as women born into them who stay, are not gullible, unintelligent dupes as observers may suppose. The human phenomena of joining and remaining in harmful groups is not unique to Mormon and Christian fundamentalist polygamy. Indeed, cult expert Robert J. Lifton conducted a ten-year study for military intelligence on Mao Tse-Tung's Chinese prisoners, which illustrated how susceptible the human psyche is to thought reform or, the popular term, brainwashing. (Robert Jay Lifton, M.D., *Thought Reform and the Psychology of Totalism*, W. W. Norton and Co. Inc. 1969)

Anyone is susceptible to thought reform and cults, and often converts are some of the very brightest of individuals. They include those who are curious seekers and those who are looking for something more in life, not being content with sitting passively as life goes on around them. Once converted, mind control takes hold as explained by cult expert Margaret Singer who wrote, "Eventually, these groups subject their followers to mind-numbing treatments that block critical and evaluative thinking and subjugate independent choice in a context of strictly enforced hierarchy." (Margaret Singer, *Cults In Our Midst, The Hidden Menace In Our Everyday Lives*, p. XX111, Josey-Bass Publishers, 1995)

Obviously this human phenomenon goes far beyond Mormon and Christian fundamentalist polygamy. There are millions of fundamentalist extremists in thousands of cults and religious movements throughout the world from Muslims to Operation Rescue (an extremist anti-abortion group that blocks women's access to abortion clinics). The Fundamentalism Project, a five-year study to examine religious movements spanning five continents, concluded with 150 scholars saying that fundamentalism is one of the fastest growing religious movements. The scholars further noted that there is a single profile in all fundamentalism. All are patriarchal, anti-feminist, anti-pluralistic and anti-liberal, with a belief that God is male, that the man in the family is the ultimate authority and that freedom makes sense only in the context of what is sacred. (Sharon Cohen, Associated Press, May 15, 1993)

In his book, *The True Believer*, Eric Hoffer notes that such groups or movements require obedience as one of the highest virtues. "Union of minds requires not only a perfect accord in the one faith, but complete submission and obedience of will." (Eric Hoffer, *The True Believer, Thoughts on The Nature of Mass Movements*, pg 117, Harper and Row, Publishers, Inc. Perennial Library edition, 1966) This is a perfect description of the polygamist woman.

The force of religion in extorting submissive and sexual behavior from girls and women in fundamentalist polygamy may not seem apparent in the stories in this book. If the women in these stories seem very removed from the religions that once consumed their lives, it is because they are. Once they began to exercise critical thinking skills, they were able to sort through the dogma, releasing the hold their religion once had on them to allow them to leave. During interviews, more than one woman stopped in the middle of a theological narrative to say, "I can't believe I ever fell for that shit."

In addition, the narratives in this book may not convey a sense of outrage that readers expect based on the stories they tell of abuse. As humans often do when they are being victimized, their minds disassociate from the acts of abuse as a mechanism in order to allow them to survive the ordeal. That same disassociation often occurs when thinking about the abuse or speaking about it. While interviewing, I recognized that many of these women were completely unable to access their innermost feelings about their abuses while they deadpanned the details. They were disassociating. The detachment to their abuse is such that many of them expressed the sentiment that their story was really no "big deal," or "nothing much." This, of course, also reflects the devaluing of themselves that occurs in polygamy.

The Oppression of Women and the Abuse of Children

Under the Taliban of Afghanistan, women's bodies were forced under the all-concealing burka. In Saudi Arabia, the religious police or Mutawin stop women if their ankles are visible beneath the mandatory black robes. In polygamy, the covering of women's bodies is also used to control them and to shame the female form under the lofty auspices of modesty.

With few roles in the world other than as "vessels to be worn out in childbirth," women in polygamy are often told it is their duty to deliver a child per year. Domestic violence and spousal rape are not acknowledged as such and result in no consequences for men who, in some polygamous communities, find polygamous police officers in league with them.

Women in polygamy become a form of currency, with children sometimes going with their mothers, and the fathers absolved from responsibility, or children automatically going to the father if the mother leaves the group. In the FLDS religion, men can be excommunicated from the church and expelled from the group while their wives and children are given to another man. Whether a women is already married or not, "releasings" (divorces) and "sealings" (marriages) from one man to another man are at the whim of the leader.

Girls are often forced into marriages at young ages to a man they may not know, often to relatives or to much older men already with wives. Trafficking of girls occurs when they are taken across state lines or into Canada and Mexico or brought to the U.S. from those countries. This is an increasing concern since polygamists translate their materials into Spanish to recruit young Mexican girls, and since a large polygamist group, the FLDS, has recently acquired property in rural Eldorado, Texas, and Mancos, Colorado. In Texas, FLDS leaders deceived the local officials by saying that their 1,300 acre purchase was for a "hunting lodge." Only when former polygamists pointed out that it appeared to be housing did FLDS leaders fess up to misleading townspeople and admit they are seeking a place to escape from prosecutors in Utah and Arizona. (See "FLDS Seek to Allay Texas Town's Fears," *Salt Lake Tribune*, 5-6-04)

With the exception of some women married to very wealthy polygamous men, the conditions that women must live in and raise their children in often involve extreme poverty even when the group holds millions of dollars in assets. Members are conditioned to believe that an impoverished life is a blessing to make them more perfected.

Children in polygamy do not know a childhood of play, having been made to work constantly. Girls are forced to become surrogate parents to younger siblings as well as to sew and cook at extremely young ages. Children in one particular group work in the religion's businesses, including in the group's dangerous coal mine, often until 10 p.m.

Education is recognized the world over, including in third world countries, as a human right. Yet thousands of polygamous children are deprived of this basic right either by being removed from school at a young age or receiving an education lacking in quality. As one polygamous leader told me, "We don't teach them the things of Babylon. They only need spelling, Hebrew, English and some computer skills so they can transcribe scripture."

The treatment boys receive often depends on family connections and ability to conform. As boys very often present competition for older men seeking marriageable girls, they are driven away to fend for themselves, stay to become the worker bees of the group or they die mysteriously. Those who leave are handicapped for assimilation into society, as they have limited education and carry the emotional scars of abandonment and abuse. In some cases they may not have birth certificates or social security numbers. If not on the streets, these boys bounce between low income jobs to survive.

With the idea that "You can all but kill a child for deliberately disobeying," girls as well as boys endure horrific beatings and other physical abuse, sometimes from the cradle. The perversion of the parent-child relationship becomes further deviant with the high incidence of sexual abuse, which includes incest as doctrine in many groups.

The abusive nature of polygamous relationships often extend to women within one household vying with one another for the affections and attention of one man. As Vicky and Rowenna explain, "What is going on with a sister-wife, or wives, is that you are sharing one penis. That's what it all revolves around."

PART TWO: The Women Who Escaped

A Lion's Grin

Thrown into a lion's den
the choice was mine to keep,
Closing my eyes I took one leap
as an angel passed me by.

Down the dark abyss
through tender arms I fall,
Razor sharp teeth growling below
the lion stalks his yard.

Hast the Lord forsaken me
when he tempted me in this den?
There is no light in here
only a lion's grin.

—Vicky Prunty, December 1991

1.

Ubi dibium ibi libertas
Where there is doubt, there is freedom
— Latin proverb

VICKY

New refugees from polygamy, Vicky Prunty and her five children were driving back to the Catholic-run women's shelter that was their temporary home when their car broke down. Calming the children, Vicky penned a note to leave on the car, "Please don't give me a ticket. I'll be back for it soon." Walking the rest of the way in the dark to the women's shelter, one child lamented, "We don't have a house. Now we don't have a car. Pretty soon we won't have nothin'."

At the age of 18 and just beginning to embark on her education at Mormon Church-owned Brigham Young University in Provo, Utah, Vicky met and fell in love with returned Mormon missionary Greg Bates. The two were married in the Mormon Temple in Salt Lake City, and Vicky ended her education to concentrate on being a wife and mother. Together the couple shared a zeal for studying their Mormon faith and its history. As they read and studied, they felt their church as it is today had significantly changed from its past. One of the changes that severely bothered the couple was its abandonment of the "law of celestial marriage" or polygamy.

The Bateses went to their local Mormon Church leaders for answers to questions but found their leaders knew precious little church history and scripture. Still seeking answers, the Bateses found Mormon fundamentalists who had a more scholarly approach and gave them books to read examining church historical and scriptural discrepancies. Through their reading, the Bateses came to believe, as did other Mormon fundamentalists, that former Mormon Church president Wilford Woodruff "signed his eternal life away with the Manifesto and plunged the church into apostasy." The fundamentalists proclaimed themselves a select people living celestial marriage as God intends. The Bateses were anxious to find a place among them. This desire was not diminished by the fact that it would also mean excommunication from the Mormon Church. This seemed a small price to pay for living a higher law.

Greg found a home for his wife and growing family with a group of Mormon fundamentalist polygamists at a place called "The Rock" in Moab, Utah. The Rock is a giant sandstone mountain. The owner, Bob Foster, and his sons dynamite-blasted the mountain to construct sections for individual families to occupy as a "refuge from Babylon." Foster is an elderly man who married two of his high school seminary (Mormon studies) students as soon as they were out of high school and one other woman. As leader of the group, he asked all who lived at The Rock to live the United Order, another belief from early Mormonism espoused as a "higher law." It involves giving all of one's resources to the community to be redistributed according to need.

While Vicky and the children lived at The Rock, Greg worked in Salt Lake City, visiting every other weekend. It was January 1988, and the infamous Mormon fundamentalist Singer/Swapp families in Heber Valley, east of Salt Lake City, had bombed a Mormon chapel to get back at the "Mormon-run state" for the earlier shooting death of their patriarch, John Singer. As the events played out in a standoff with the FBI, Utah police officer Fred House was killed. With the Swapp men now in prison, Greg saw fit to help the widow Singer and her family, who was now destitute of male leadership. While living at the Singer/Swapp farm, Greg met a young woman named Marlene, who often visited the Singer and Swapp families. Marlene would become Greg's second wife and Vicky's first sister-wife.

All of her life, Marlene's father had told her, "You're too pretty and too good to be a second wife." Second place wasn't what Marlene intended, but she relented to Greg's persuasion.

When Vicky first met Marlene, she was so nervous that later Marlene told her she thought Vicky had a speech impediment. At the wedding, Vicky, pregnant with her fourth child, placed Marlene's hand into the hand of her husband and gave Marlene to Greg. Vicky feels she lost her partnership with her husband from that day on. Later she would ask, "How can I give this woman to you when I don't own her?" The reception that followed the wedding was lavish. Due to the family's wish to hide their polygamous lifestyle, Vicky remained in the background, the only family member without flowers, as guests greeted the happy couple. She was told to pose as "a friend of the family."

Life at The Rock was short lived. Vicky and her children soon joined Greg and Marlene in Salt Lake City. They later moved to St. George, Utah, then back to Salt Lake. Wherever they lived, they found the company of other Mormon polygamist fundamentalists, each independent family or group having its own doctrinal slant on polygamy, such as one group in St. George that advocated a "Sarah Doctrine," a belief taken from Sarah of the Bible who set rules for Abraham's concubine, Hagar.

A color photograph of Greg and his two wives shows Vicky, hair shining in the bright sunshine, sitting on Greg's lap while Marlene rests her arms on his shoulder from behind, all three smiling happily and dressed in clothes that would not distinguish them as polygamous. Only Greg wore the long-sleeved, long-legged Mormon temple garments from Mormonism's past.

Many of these Mormon fundamentalist men write books and scripture at great length, most of which concern polygamy. A scripture written by Greg reads, "If the wife is subject to her husband's law, then she truly has no right to refuse his taking other wives besides her in her lifetime. She is, after all, under his dominion. If she had the right to refuse, she would then have the right to withhold from her own husband (whom she should love more than herself!) his exaltation! That is not a right granted to a wife!" In other passages Greg expounds on the evils of feminism. Women in Mormon polygamy spend much of their free time reading these books and scriptures as well as the Bible. They also study Mormon Church history and the standard works of Mormonism, which include the *Book of Mormon, Doctrine & Covenants*, and *Pearl of Great Price*. Other books read by polygamists are the works written by Ogden Kraut, a prolific fundamentalist polygamist who died in the summer of 2002. Vicky feels that, "The women don't think; they don't even know how to think. They read and read and it's a brainwashing."

A basic right that most polygamous wives lose is the right to vote. Greg rhetorically wrote, "What need have women to vote if they are in subjection to the law of their husband?" Despite these men's means of denying women selfhood and independence, some wives are permitted work of one kind or another since the husband's wages, if he has any, are spread thinly among his wives and many children.

While some polygamous women publicly profess happiness and ardently defend plural marriage, Vicky observed, "They change their minds every other day, going back and forth, much like Emma [Mormon Church founder Joseph Smith's first wife] did." Vicky says that she has never seen any truly happy families within these polygamous groups. "Every man has his favorite wife," she explains. "It causes a lot of hurt."

Greg had his favorite wife as well, and it was Marlene. Vicky emphasizes that she deeply loved Marlene as a sister-wife, but she was having problems sharing her husband. To Vicky the situation was, "a way in which he used sex as abuse." They each took turns sleeping with Greg but if Vicky displeased Greg in any way, he would give her night(s) to Marlene and tell Vicky that she could not return to his bed until she repented.

Greg often responded to her questions and her feelings of unhappiness with his own favorite quote, "Do not voice your opinion if it is contrary to mine." Vicky made a poster of the quote and hung it on her wall as a reminder. She worked hard at being "meek and obedient" and to "reverence her head," which meant that he was her leader to whom she must bow. In another of Greg's scriptures, he illustrates his relationship with God, Jesus and his wives: "Fraternal oneness is horizontal; marital oneness is vertical."

Vicky felt that Greg's verbal and emotional abuse worked to diminish her as a human. He made fun of her prayers and the way she ate. He would ridicule her when they were with other fundamentalist members. Because of her "rebelliousness," he would tell others that she was possessed with demons. It was only when Vicky saw Greg's mistreatment of Marlene that she recognized his behavior as abusive. There were times when Vicky's unhappiness was so profound that she would cry uncontrollably, not remember her name, or find herself somewhere in the car and not know how she got there. Greg would use those situations to convince her that she was possessed, and he and other polygamous men would attempt to "cast out the demons from her."

Eventually Vicky left Greg and Marlene, taking her children with her. "I got tired of being a martyr and I thought maybe he was the one possessed with demons," she says. "I also decided if this was celestial marriage, I'd rather be happy in hell than be miserable in heaven." In discussing child visitation and support with Vicky, Greg explained to her, "You are mine to dispose of unless I decide you're worthy. You belong to my family kingdom. God may tell me in this lifetime that you've repented, then I'll take you back. You'll be cut off if you don't repent. You may be sensing you can't get rid of me; like a dog trying to rid himself of his master, it's impossible. You'll always be coming back." In December 1992, their eleven-year marriage ended in divorce.

Choices, resources and aid are scarce for a single mother of five who has no marketable skills or education. Vicky had lost more than a husband and sister-wife. She had also lost a community and security. The only people who offered help were another independent polygamist family, Christopher and his wives, Jackie and Marcie. Not knowing where to go and feeling the need to have a father for her children, she agreed to become a third and "full wife" of Christopher. Now feeling wanted, loved, supported and secure, she was drawn into her second polygamous marriage. Vicky and Christopher wed themselves to one another with their own vows. Many independent polygamous couples marry this way, believing that "At the right time we will be sealed to one another by the correct authority." Vicky knew how Jackie felt and would continue to see in Jackie what she herself had suffered in the role of first wife. During this union, Vicky "multiplied Christopher's seed" by giving birth to her sixth child.

Christopher believed in living without material and worldly goods. This literally meant living on the floor without beds, chairs, sofas or many other household necessities. Much of the money the family received was sent to help the poor in Argentina, where Christopher had once served a Mormon mission. Vicky, however, had furniture from her previous marriage and the trend of using furniture caught on.

One morning when the three wives were together, Christopher made an announcement. He no longer wanted to live polygamy. He would keep Jackie as his wife since she was first. He then admitted that he had not entered into polygamy for religious reasons. He had done it strictly for his ego and had grown tired of the charade. Jackie was thrilled. Marcie and Vicky were horrified. They had given birth to his children and all their children were half-brothers and sisters. He told Vicky that for $100 a month he would expect visitation. If she didn't want him to see his child, then he wouldn't pay anything.

After moving about for five years, (returning to Christopher once and later getting a protective order against him) Vicky found herself with six children, homeless and with no one to turn to. She and her children sought refuge at the YWCA shelter in Salt Lake City, which would allow them to stay for only 30 days.

After their stay at the shelter, Vicky moved with the children to the Catholic-run women's shelter. Once there, she found that at age 11, her eldest son was too old to stay due to close quarters and shared bathrooms, so Vicky made the difficult choice of sending him to live with his father, Greg.

Her experience with other Mormon fundamentalists convinced Vicky that there had to be many other women who wanted to escape from polygamy but had not because they were not aware of resources available. Another reason they do not leave is that polygamous husbands verbally and emotionally abuse wives who consider leaving, threatening them with death, taking their children away from them and having them committed to mental institutions. In some cases, wives who have tried to flee have been pursued by members of the group. "Women have no safety net and no control over the poverty and homelessness waiting if they leave," Vicky explains. Regarding her own situation, she says, "I would feel so overwhelmed and be in such desperation that I'd think about prostitution at the same time thinking, `I know I could never do that.' But that's how your mind works in that situation. Other times you feel like you're in a public arena being torn apart and no one comes to help." It became a goal for Vicky to start an organization to help women leaving polygamy, a goal she was to see to fruition as one of the founding members of Tapestry Against Polygamy.

Greg was paying $630 monthly in child support for their five children, but it was an amount that would barely cover rent. In addition, Vicky had no money for a deposit, which meant she couldn't lease an apartment. Welfare wouldn't give her money for a deposit unless she could show that she had a lease and enough money to pay for first and last months' rent. She would have to come up with a deposit on her own. "It was very hard for me to beg; but I did because it wasn't for me, it was for my children," she says.

During the time she was homeless, Vicky sought help from the Mormon Church. She was aware of the Mormon Church policy that bishops (similar to a pastor but an unpaid lay person who serves for a limited time) should give help and aid to members and nonmembers living within their ward (similar to a parish) boundaries. She felt that by being a good mother she was deserving, so she ventured to ask the Mormon bishop for help. Pointing to the candy dish on his desk he replied, "I can't do anything for you, but you can take some candy for your kids."

Finally, after going to eight different individuals to ask for help, she collected enough money to pay the deposit on a small apartment.

On numerous occasions she asked one bishop if she could be rebaptized but his answer was always the same, "You haven't repented enough." The missionaries informed her that her transgressions were so great that to be rebaptized, she would need the approval of the First Presidency of the Mormon Church. The members of the ward who knew of her past advised her not to speak of it. Over the phone, a Relief Society President (the ward women's group president) suggested that she "take in ironing at night to make ends meet." An already exhausted Vicky cut the conversation short and wept.

Today, Vicky lives with her six children in a rented house in Salt Lake City, where she proudly points out the furnishings she purchased at yard sales. Her kitchen doors are an art gallery of her children's masterpieces. The surroundings are spartan, but the family has what they need to make a house a home. They survive on meager child-support and food-stamps each month while she volunteers for Tapestry.

In speaking of the unusual circumstances of her life, she often rolls her eyes in a gesture of disbelief at the absurd. The topic that most affects her emotions is that of her children. She is a ferociously committed mother.

For a while after she left, Greg and Marlene prayed for her. Their prayers were for her death so that she could "blood atone" for leaving them. While at Greg's, the children are not allowed to call her "mom." They have to call her Vicky. They come home from court-ordered visitation with Greg and complain that Marlene's children call their mother "V-yulky." "My children have to endure mental abuse. They cry when they have to go to Greg's home because they say they don't like Dad saying bad things about me," she says. "He's very authoritarian; he spanks them. Once he thought Marlene's baby was possessed because the baby kept crying. He ended up making the baby's mouth bleed with his ring as he tried to stop the baby from crying [by moving his hand over the baby's face to exorcise demons]. I worry the whole time the kids are there, especially my little ones." Her oldest son lived with Greg until recently. He lived with Vicky and his siblings again for a while and then moved out on his own. Through another relationship that did not result in marriage, she has added another child to the family she struggles to care for.

Vicky has come to terms with religion by avoiding it entirely. Face radiant and eyes shining, she says, "I no longer have tunnel vision to follow a `straight and narrow path' of anyone or anything. I think for myself now." She laughs saying, "The Mormon Church wanted me to repent. Maybe they should repent. Polygamy is their legacy and they won't take responsibility for what that legacy continues to do to women and children."

Greg and Marlene are the only fictitious names in this story.

2.

*SATORI—The Buddhist concept of
letting go of illusion and mistaken belief.*

ROWENNA

Today, Rowenna Erickson lives alone in her newly built brick home just behind her sister's two-story farm house in the Salt Lake Valley. But for 11 years, she shared her sister's home. And for 37 years, she and her sister shared the same husband.

In the Mormon fundamentalist polygamist group known as the Kingstons, the two sisters had married well. Their husband was a son of Charles Eldon Kingston, the patriarch and leader who began The Latter-day Church of Christ in 1935, just four years before Rowenna was born. But in spite of their kinship to the upper echelons of the leadership, following the religious requirements of polygamy would not be such an easy task for this particular branch of the Kingston family.

Rowenna and her siblings were raised with a background unique to the others in the church. Unlike other members, who were all former Mormons, their father was Lutheran. It was a background that provided them with other ways of thinking. And Rowenna was absorbing a great deal of those other ways from her father. "My father loved my dogmatic Mormon mother, so he went along with her; but at the same time, he provided a window in my thinking," says Rowenna. "He liked the Kingston people; and, though he never joined the Mormon Church or this new split-off religion itself, he sat on its board of directors. It was a position he held until his death while always being called the 'Judas' of the board."

The estimated 2,000 members of The Latter-day Church of Christ are isolated and forced to live in deprivation. "The poverty is so extreme because the women have to support themselves and their children on so little while being commanded to have a baby a year," says Rowenna. "The higher-up Kingstons have access to the money; but, like everyone, they're taught that it belongs to God, so their mind set is that they can't use it."

At one point, wallpaper was ordered torn from the walls of people's ramshackle homes. "No one could even have any pictures hanging," remembers Rowenna. "Everyone had to live as Christ did, as he was born in the manger without the extravagances of the world." At times, members are made to fast every other day and adults ordered to go without sex for six weeks at a time, as the prophet requests, to test their obedience. Mantras, or "Memory Gems" as they are called, must be repeated twice daily by all members at the same exact time.

Rowenna still remembers one Memory Gem: "With my firm resolve and fixed purpose, I give my all to the Lord—my time, my talents, all that I hope to be—to the establishment of the Kingdom of God on Earth."

She shakes her head remembering hearing of a time before her birth when everyone, including children, was forced to eat radishes for an entire day, and of another time when all possessions were taken away and given back one by one as the leader felt they had been earned. "What clever control it was," she says.

Members are strictly forbidden to mix with those in "Babylon," and most girls are pulled from public school by age 14. Boys are allowed to finish high school and go on to college, with the leader of the church choosing their career paths. "My husband obtained a law degree, but he was never allowed to practice law," says Rowenna. "He was forced to work in the church's shoe shop."

The leaders of the church profess a belief that the Kingston family line traces back to Jesus Christ, and therefore they possess holy blood. The family intermarries in order to keep this bloodline "pure." It is not uncommon for half-brothers and sisters to marry, uncles and nieces to marry, aunts and nephews to marry, etc. Thus several genetic diseases and mutations appear within the church's members: dwarfism; various genital and congenital defects; fused limbs; no fingernails; numerous mental illnesses; spina bifida and microcephalous, a condition causing the head to be very small and the child to endure seizures, along with being mentally impaired.

Throughout her life, Rowenna has observed the marriages and births of every individual in this tight-knit community. She shows painful emotion in relating the histories of people she has always known. "I'll never forgive Merlin Kingston for killing his second wife, Carolyn," she says. "He starved that helpless, sick woman to death." Carolyn had been shot during a robbery of one of the Kingston businesses. The bullet struck her head and though an operation was performed to remove the bullet, she was left with brain damage. According to Rowenna, Merlin was obsessed that Carolyn had also been sexually assaulted in the robbery. In a religiously inspired attempt to heal and purify her, Merlin withheld her medicine, food and all liquids. Carolyn died as a result, without any investigation by state authorities. "She was also Merlin's niece," says Rowenna. "He also married another one of his nieces. Several of the eight children from that marriage were born without fingernails." Rowenna further tells how one of Merlin's sons married three of his half-sisters. "Two children from one wife are dwarves, another has a dwarf, and still another had an infant whose limbs were fused together when it was born. It died soon after birth." Church leaders characterize birth defects as God's punishment of mothers who are not sufficiently submissive to their husbands or faithful to the church.

Women, men and children work for the church's many businesses located throughout Utah and surrounding states. They provide an essentially free labor force that has helped make the church a $200 million organization. As a young girl, Rowenna worked in one of the church-owned general stores, making 35 cents an hour in the form of a service slip (scrip) that could be used only in other church stores. The remainder of her wages were turned over to the church's "co-op," short for Davis Cooperative Society, which was patterned after the early Mormon Church's United Order. "We were told to sacrifice everything for the kingdom to the point that if we found a penny in the street we were to turn it in," says Rowenna. "We were deprived of knowing anything about money or having any experience with it."

Rowenna's parents sacrificed and followed every tenet of the religion except polygamy, which was introduced into the religion after they were married. (Intermarriage was introduced in the 1950s by the group's second leader, John Ortell Kingston, who modeled it on the breeding practices of his dairy herd. He believed it was needed to keep the bloodline pure.) Not living in polygamy was a major omission on their part. The leader would never allow a girl to marry a man who was not a member of the faith, but Rowenna's father could never stand the idea of polygamy. "There was a split in the family that we children were always aware of," says Rowenna. "For my Dad, family was first and for my Mom, the Kingdom of God was first. It was a real conflict for me."

The split between the parents extended to their daughters' futures as well. "My mother was always unhappy that she could never live in polygamy and she wanted it for us girls," Rowenna remembers. "All the while, my Dad was adamantly against it." His wishes, however, were no match for the collusion between their mother with her prodding and the indoctrination by the religion to become polygamous wives. "We were forever told to get in a state of mind that we'd marry anyone that the Lord wanted us to marry," she says.

Rowenna's older sister married as the first wife of a man she was very much in love with, and the new husband would tease and joke with Rowenna. Seven years into the marriage, he called Rowenna and told her he would like to talk to her. "I said, 'The answer is yes,'" she remembers. "I knew what he was calling about; and though I didn't love him, I just thought, 'Let's get on with it.'" She was 20 years old.

Her sister made the wedding cake; and within two years, Rowenna bore her first child, delivered by her sister who was a trained midwife. She would have her first three children within three years and two days.

There was no romance in Rowenna's marriage as she, and apparently her husband, felt the union was nothing more than living a duty. "I could never fall in love with my sister's husband, and I felt guilty for sleeping with him," she says. "In my life, I've never known love with someone of the opposite sex."

Besides lacking love, the marriage lacked communication. She lived on food stamps in dire poverty while her husband worked for the church, helping them to amass millions. "He never interacted with me on any level," she says. "When I was pregnant, he never asked when I was due or if I needed anything. I couldn't even buy shoes for my eight kids, and he worked in the shop where there were hundreds of shoes. Oh my hell, I was lonely."

During one period of time when Rowenna and her eight children lived in a separate residence from her sister, they were crammed into a two-bedroom shack in a run-down part of Salt Lake City known as Swede Town. "I also had my mom living with us and I was taking in kids [baby-sitting] and collecting cans to recycle for money," she remembers. One day Rowenna noticed that two backyard sheds the children played in appeared on the verge of collapse. With only a sledge hammer, the tiny five-foot-two inch woman poured her anger and frustration into the complete dismantling of the sheds, including the concrete flooring. "I beat the cement into pieces with that hammer and tore it up from the ground with my bare hands."

As a rule in this religion, multiple marriages are kept secret even from other members. Rowenna chose her last name from the phone book, as do many other women. Some choose a name from a distant relative. Children in the Kingston group are never told who their fathers are for fear that a polygamous man will be found out and prosecuted by local government; although, with a few token exceptions, the state of Utah has long turned a blind eye to those practicing polygamy.

Many mothers tell their children that their father has gone to serve in the army, is a truck driver or is working in another state, but that he will return some day. Women often live on welfare, telling social workers that they got pregnant by an unknown truck driver who was passing through town. "I remember one time seeing two little boys arguing about whose father was the strongest. It turned out they had the same father," she says. "The fathers can't acknowledge their children, leaving the kids so deprived. It's child abuse. One of those boys later committed suicide."

Rowenna's children were no different in not knowing who their father was. One of her children's cousins, however, figured it out and let the secret out to the other children. "Once they all knew, my children still couldn't call him 'father,' and it hurt the kids on both sides," she says. "And it hurt them that they had to say that their own half-brothers and sisters were 'cousins.'"

Lest anyone catch on to the family arrangement, neither set of children could bring playmates over during the time that the families lived in a combined residence, and Rowenna had to keep to herself. "While we were all under one roof, I was an embarrassment. My sister could know the neighbors who weren't members, but I couldn't," she says.

While living with her own pain in the relationship, Rowenna watched helplessly as her sister plunged into the depths of depression. The two had always been close, never knowing sibling rivalry. Rowenna's sister had doted on her, waiting through the births of two brothers for her arrival. On the one hand, she wanted nothing more than for Rowenna to have a successful marriage. On the other, she was deeply in love with her husband.

"It's as though your husband is having an affair and you're supposed to be happy about it. If you're not happy, it's because you have fallen out of favor with God and let Satan in," explains Rowenna. "It's another crisis when the other wife or wives start having children. My sister was having feelings she didn't know existed. These feelings shocked her, and she no longer knew how to have a relationship with her husband." Then, one day after ironing through the morning, her sister came to her and told Rowenna that everything was all right. She would not be having these feelings any longer. "She came to that point because her spirit had been broken," says Rowenna. "Just like a horse. They broke her."

Within her world of all-consuming loneliness, Rowenna remembers that in order to live through each day, she couldn't allow herself to think about whether she was happy or unhappy. "Of course you always have to say that you're happy, but inside you have to know your limits, live on the surface and never touch under the surface," she says. But a distinct cognitive dissonance nagged at her carefully-constructed facade. "Everything felt so wrong, and yet I was constantly being told it was right and godly. So I was overwhelmed with a feeling of guilt. After a while, living a lie gets on your nerves."

With an interest in alternative medicine and particularly in hypnosis, Rowenna began taking hypnotherapy classes. "I'd always known the mind had power and potential. I discovered a teacher named Virgil Hayes. He taught me the mind's power." She credits Hayes with also giving her the personal fortitude to get out of polygamy. "He taught me all the hallmarks of brainwashing, and though he couldn't know it at the time, he was talking about the Kingstons."

The last straw for Rowenna came with two incidents occurring within the group. She was witness to the four-day, nonstop physical torture and brutalization of a women carried out by the woman's husband in order to "humble" her. The next incident was the arrival in her mail of an anonymously-sent envelope containing pornographic photos taken by a leader of the church of himself and one of his wives. The combination of what she was living, seeing and hearing became more than she could keep inside, prompting her to fire off a scathing letter comparing the church leaders to "Saddam and Hitler." It was an action that lead to her being excommunicated from the religion she had given her life to, a consequence that made her feel both "relieved and afraid." Still she did not leave her polygamous marriage until three year later, when she was 57.

A few months after the end of her marriage, Rowenna attended a community panel discussion of child sexual abuse within the Mormon Church. While listening to the speakers, she felt their descriptions and pain resonate with familiarity. "I came to realize the sexual abuse that had happened to me in living polygamy," she says. "These men have control of women's bodies, whether naked or clothed, and women have nothing."

Rowenna and her sister remain very close. The husband they once shared continues to work for the Co-op, providing her minimal financial support. Her children are grown, have left the Kingston group and are leading productive lives. Her life is very full, working as a founding member of Tapestry Against Polygamy and caring for her grandchildren.

In keeping with her reputation for outspokenness against the lifestyle she endured for too long, Rowenna says, "You can tell a man dreamed all this up. Polygamy is one big eternal fuck."

3.

There are no righteous societies;
there are simply different degrees of depravity.
—Howard Bloom, *The Lucifer Principle*

LILLIAN

When Lillian Bowles' parents met for the first time, her father already had four wives. But it wasn't difficult for her mother to make the leap from Mormon girl to polygamist wife since, as a faithful Latter-day Saint, she already believed that she would have to live polygamy someday. Lillian's father, George, had once been a Mormon himself; but in finding the Allred group, whose religion is the Apostolic United Brethren (AUB), he became convinced that he'd found the "fullness of the truth."

As a dedicated male in the AUB, George rose quickly in the hierarchy to become a councilman under the prophet, Owen Allred. "George ended up with eight total wives but two left him," says Lillian. "I grew up with six mothers and 39 siblings, but only six of us were my mom's kids and two of my dad's wives never had children."

While George maintained the same home in Riverton, Utah, throughout his life with his two childless wives, and continues to do so, his wives who bore children were shuffled all over the Salt Lake Valley. Sometimes they lived together under one very large roof, sometimes together with added families and other times the mothers were in separate housing with their own children. There were still other periods of time when children were interchanged between mothers. "One mother,

Susan, was mentally ill but she had fourteen children. Her sister, Naomi, was also married to my father," says Lillian. "Because of her mental state, Susan was treated worse than an animal and always had to live in a barn or a shed with her kids farmed out to other mothers. She died in her 50s looking ancient and with no teeth."

Lillian's childhood was marked by one overriding emotion: "I felt unsafe my whole life." Her earliest memories are when she, her mother and five siblings lived on their own. "Mom was always working as a nurse's aide, so we'd get dropped off at Naomi's house. But Naomi hated my mother, so she took it out on us kids," remembers Lillian. "I'd hide behind the couch and wait for my mother to come back. With so many kids, you try to stay out of the way."

The children were sometimes home-schooled by another mother, and at other times were enrolled in the AUB school taught by members who themselves had very little education. "The home-schooling was a joke. They didn't know what they were doing at the AUB school, but they taught us anyway."

Though Lillian's father looked at his position in the AUB church as a calling from God, he harbored numerous disagreements with the prophet. "Some men in the church get their own United Order set up with their own families, then they recruit other members into it," explains Lillian. "So that's what George did—I could never call him father—but he went a little further. We were taught to strive to be 'lifted up,' and we really believed we would be, because we were doing it right."

George would hold meetings of his own after the regular AUB meetings, and soon 15 other men had become a part of what he would call "The Order." "They made it similar to the Mormon Church's priesthood. They were going to live the highest laws," says Lillian. "The men had to wear white, button-down shirts and the women wore long sleeves and long dresses. They hated it that Owen [Allred] allowed members to roll up their sacred garments and wear shorter dresses."

Every Saturday, her mother would disappear to work in The Order's temple. "One time she came home and told me that if she ever broke her temple ordinances, she hoped someone would kill her in blood atonement," remembers Lillian. "That was a devastating thing for me, as a child, to hear."

Another dictate in The Order was that no one was to talk to "gentiles," meaning anyone who was not a member of the AUB. "I never talked to anyone outside the Allred group until I was 14 and got a job," says Lillian.

Lillian says her mother would always hand her paycheck over to George, who used it as he wished. "Our only source of food was from the garbage bins in the back of grocery stores, and it was my mom's designated job to get it," she says. "One of us kids would stand watch, and mom or one of us would get inside and find the food. It was scary because we didn't want to get caught. It would take four to five hours to clean the food up when we got it back home."

At one time, the mothers and their children were moved into a large, L-shaped complex in Sandy, Utah, a suburb of Salt Lake. Six other polygamist families in her father's order moved into the large house as well, each with multiple wives and numerous children.

Because of their large numbers, the adults were paranoid that people would notice that polygamists were living in the structure. To avoid questioning neighbors, the children were instructed to play inside the courtyard where they could not be seen. "We had five acres but we couldn't go out there," she says. "And when we went to church, we all had to go in a school bus."

While living in this structure, Lillian's nine-year-old brother died while climbing an electric pole. He lost his balance and, as he began to fall, he grabbed a power line and was electrocuted. The tragedy caused a marked change in Lillian's once outgoing and busy mother. "From then on, I took the role of making her better and looking after my siblings." But expecting a child to raise other children is not only grossly unfair, it's impossible. "I remember that one sister from another mother would fondle us while we were in bed," says Lillian. "In environments like that, everyone is a victim in survival mode with no guidelines."

A teen brother from yet another mother would take six-year-old Lillian into a little room in the basement and molest her. "That house had so many little rooms in the basement," says Lillian. Another brother was molesting and physically abusing all of the younger children, including Lillian, whom he raped. "He would throw us across the room by our hair," she says. "Now as an adult, he's in prison for rape of a child and an adult."

The younger children complained about the abuse to the adults in the family to no avail. "Our family just downplayed what was happening," recalls Lillian. "So I'd think my family was weird, but that it wasn't that bad."

The families lived in this communal hellhole for five years. Their stay ended abruptly after the septic tank overflowed, and the men dug ditches to drain the sewage away from the house and into a nearby field. "An attorney was building a house in that field; and he turned us in to the health board, which kicked us all out of the house," remembers Lillian. "The grown-ups told us that we were being persecuted because we were polygamists."

Lillian began noticing that the men in her father's special order had motives other than religious zealotry. "If a man served George and was faithful, he would get to marry one of George's daughters. And he had a lot of daughters," she says. "One man, Jerry, would get revelations about which daughter he should marry; then he'd badger the girl."

When Jerry turned his attentions on 12-year-old Lillian, she recoiled. "He began pinching my cheeks," she says. "I just hated him." One day, when he went to pinch them, she slapped his hand away and took off. The rejection enraged Jerry and he ran after Lillian. "He was going to beat the hell out of me," she says. "He screamed at me that I didn't have the right as a child or as a woman to reject him." Later, Jerry told Lillian's father what had happened. In response, her father punished her and told her that she should never "disrespect an Elder."

Lillian was also getting hints from a sister's husband that he was interested in her. "It was my 13th birthday, and he bought me a wedding cake. It freaked me out. These men were all way older and were all married to one of my sisters, but I was resigned that it was my fate."

When 28-year-old Scott joined her father's order, Lillian saw her first glimmer of hope of avoiding forced marriage to a man her father's age. Though still much older than herself, Scott seemed like a boy in comparison to the others. He already had one wife and was interested in Lillian's older sister for a second wife, so Lillian became a chaperone as he and her sister courted. "I watched his first wife go through such a hard time seeing him court my sister, while feeling jealous about it myself," she says. "Scott would tell me to wait awhile, then he'd marry me as the third wife."

Lillian was still waiting for her turn to marry Scott when she overheard him talking to her sister. "He was saying, 'I love my first wife and I love your sister, but you're the one I really love.' He had said that same thing to me. What a liar," she remembers now with a laugh. "Women in polygamy have to believe those lies in order to hang in there. They have to believe they're the one he truly wants to be with."

Lillian's mother was less than thrilled with Scott's attentions to two of her daughters at one time and told him to stay away from Lillian. He in turn went to her father. "George told my mom to mind her own business and that it wasn't her place to tell a priesthood holder what to do." In the end, neither sister married Scott.

Lillian's mother soon moved herself and her children into a rundown trailer next to the AUB church. Lillian, age 14, began working on the assembly line of a Salt Lake-area medical supply company owned by the Colorado City polygamists. There she got to know several non-polygamists or "outsiders" and became uncomfortably aware that her education was lacking. When she reached her 16th birthday, she bought a car and enrolled in night school without her father's knowledge. She continued to be immersed in her culture and religion and eventually became involved with a boy her age who was also a member of the AUB. When they were both 17, he asked Lillian's father if he could marry her. "My dad thought Gary would join his order so he agreed," she says. "I was the first of George's daughters to become a first wife. I got married and moved out, but Gary made me quit night school."

Dashing Lillian's hopes for a home of her own, Gary bought a home with his parents and moved her into only one of the bedrooms. She tried to be happy in spite of the living arrangements with his promise that he would never take a second wife without her full agreement, something she told herself she would never give. "Within four months of our wedding, he started talking about a second wife," she says. "And it never quit. In priesthood meetings, he kept asking about other girls; then he would come home and tell me who he had in mind."

Gary continued to pursue second wife possibilities as Lillian gave birth to their first child and then their second.

Then a plague of nightmares began to invade Lillian's nights. "I'd wake up in a cold sweat from dreams of being force-fed rats. I would wake up and I could smell the rats," she recalls. "These weren't normal bad dreams. They were different. And then insomnia set in."

One day during church, Lillian and one of her half-sisters went to the car to talk. Lillian began telling the sister about her dreams. "My sister started crying and hyperventilating. She said that another of our sisters had recently told her the same thing," says Lillian. "But she wouldn't tell me which sister because she promised she wouldn't tell. The whole idea freaked me out, so I told her and Gary never to speak to me about my dreams again."

At the time, Lillian was too overloaded by more immediate crises in her life. Her son had just been diagnosed as autistic, and her marriage was ending—falling victim to the religious dictates of polygamy. "Gary told me he was set on marrying a second wife. I got suicidal until I talked to another woman—in fact one of the prophet's daughters, who had left her polygamist husband and the AUB," she says. "She was an example of leaving, but it took two years for me to work up to it. Finally, I told Gary I was divorcing him. I left the AUB and took off my garments."

It was at this time that Tapestry Against Polygamy was beginning to form, so Lillian made her way to the early planning meetings. The camaraderie she found, combined with a focus on something bigger than any one individual, sustained her while she moved on with her life, working and caring for her children. "You leave and there's no help. That's why I wanted to help Tapestry organize," she explains. "We have the same problems as other single moms, but there's a twist with bigger dynamics to it."

Still, as Lillian gained a foothold in a new world on the "outside," panic attacks began to grip her. Then came flashbacks in fragmented scenes. "In these snippets, I see the house where my dad has always lived. I'm down inside the basement wearing a white dress, and the men in The Order are all there. They're wearing their white shirts," she says. "I'm forced to eat rats, and I'm raped by my father and other members of The Order."

After these memories started flooding Lillian's waking hours, she felt compelled to talk to the other sister who she'd been told had been having the dreams. After pleading with the one sister who was their confidante, the two were finally brought together. "It was Rachel. She was Susan's daughter and I hadn't seen her in years," says Lillian. "Since confiding to our sister, Rachel had been to see a therapist. She was strong; and now after hearing about me, she wanted to confront Owen."

Rachel also was angry at how her mother had been treated through the years; so she sent word to Owen that if he didn't agree to a meeting with herself and her mother, she would expose the abuse to the media, as well as his knowledge of it and other things he would regret coming into the open. Within hours, Owen called the women in. They told him only the essence of what they wanted to talk about, stating that they would meet him for an in-depth discussion at another time but only with other people present. "We wanted witnesses to hear everything so he couldn't deny things later," says Lillian. "Before we left, he told us that he should have intervened, as he knew what was happening, but that he didn't because a man's family is his own property."

At the second meeting, several individuals arrived as witnesses, including one of Owen's eight wives. "She was a midwife and was there to determine whether we were lying or not," says Lillian. "I didn't talk. I flipped out when Rachel started talking. I was hitting my eyes, and they had to stop because they thought they'd have to take me to the hospital." The meeting ended with a decision to convene an AUB court, similar to a Mormon excommunication court.

Council members were sitting in a circle with arms folded as George was put on trial for his sins. "His only response was, 'I'm sorry you think I've hurt you. I never did these things,'" says Lillian. "Then he quoted the Bible about Judas betraying Jesus." At the end of the court, George was kicked out of the council; yet he is still a member of the AUB and still attends church. Owen Allred never did or said anything to the other men in George's order.

Another sister who is a talented artist has begun drawing disturbing pictures. She tells Lillian they're only pictures from her bad dreams. Lillian hasn't said anything to her about where the dreams might be coming from or what they could mean. Lillian and Rachel do not see each other or talk with one another anymore.

At this point in her life, Lillian is resistant to therapy. "I'm working hard on my career. I bought a house and I'm trying to move on," she says. "But sometimes a face or a scene surfaces when I let down a little bit, and boom—I'm there."

She continues to support Tapestry, helping others who are escaping polygamy find services such as housing and jobs. "It's the sickest way of living ever; and women do it for a ticket to heaven, thinking the hell they live now is worth it," she says. "I look back and recognize the signs of a cult: fear and the parade of 'how happy people are' bullshit. They're conditioned to say that. It's what you're taught because if you don't say you're happy, you'll go to hell. They don't recognize that. It took me a long time."

4.

I dwell in possibility.
—Emily Dickinson

STACY

At the developmental stage when many children create an imaginary friend to accompany them through their lonely hours, Stacy Erickson, Rowenna's daughter, instead created an imaginary father since the Kingston group she belonged to did not allow children to know who their fathers are for fear of prosecution.

Stacy was led to believe her father was away in the army. The fragile blonde child imagined him to be a fantastic hero who was loving and protective. Some day, the daddy she longed for would come back from the army and save her from the confusion and fear surrounding her life in the Kingston group.

But by the second grade, her dashing father image perished as surely as though a man of flesh had died in some faraway war. "I remember it clearly when Marie, who was two years older than me, explained it to me in my backyard," says Stacy. "She had unraveled the mystery of her own father's identity and had also discovered mine. The same bossy, scary man who I'd always known as my uncle was actually my dad. I knew she was right, and I don't remember ever being so disappointed."

As convoluted, confusing and painful as it was, the issue surrounding her paternity did not seem odd to Stacy in later years. "I thought, 'Didn't all families go through this?'" she remembers. "They did in my circle of peers. I didn't have any close friends who weren't members of the Kingston group." In fact, her best friends were also her cousins on her father's side. "We're all related in the Kingston group."

She was born the fifth of her mother's eight children and the 11th of her father's 14 children, born to two wives who were also sisters. Her half-siblings were always allowed to call him "Dad"; but Stacy and her mother's other children would call him only by his first name, even after learning he was their father. Stacy and her immediate siblings were never to accept him as their father. "We kids dreaded it when it was our mother's turn to have him over to our house," she says. "There was never a good relationship with him, and it got worse after we knew who he really was."

Stacy obediently attended the church's Sunday School, but she says her mother's children never fit in. "We were naughty in church. When I was ten years old, we were supposed to read the *Book of Mormon*," laughs Stacy. "So we said we did, but never did." The blue-blooded Kingstons looked down on the half-Kingston family, believing that Stacy's grandfather had tainted the pureness of that particular Kingston blood line. Other members of the religion, who had no Kingston blood, considered the children superior to themselves. These two conflicting messages gave Stacy and her siblings a crack to squeeze through in search of their own definition of self and place.

In the early years of the Kingston group, the male members wore only blue coveralls with a string tied around the waist. Women wore plain, long blue dresses with no pockets. They later abandoned this way of dressing to wear clothing that would not identify them as polygamists. Most members' attire now appears about 20 years behind contemporary fashion and is often noticeably dirty.

Stacy went to public school with other Kingston children who, while believing "outside" children were inferior, were also trying to blend in with them. The boys from the church were allowed to finish high school, but most of the girls were pulled out by their teens in order to marry as plural wives.

From the time she was 12 years old, Stacy worked for the group's businesses. The percentage of her pay she was allowed to keep was deposited in the group bank account; she would receive a statement telling her how much she had. "All jobs were called 'stewardships,' and we got a spending card that indicated our deposit balance that we could spend in the other businesses owned by the Kingstons," she explains. "But we understood that the leaders could take your money to use for the church anytime they wanted. And anyway, you don't really ever want to spend down your account because your amount is a measure of your worthiness. The more you have, the better you are." If members want cash to use on the outside, they have to go to the leaders and provide a valid reason for spending currency in outside businesses. The leaders often reject such a request.

The Kingston group has assets estimated at more than $200 million, with multiple businesses and land holdings throughout Utah including a law office, the Washakie Ranch, Amusement Games, A-1 Disposal, Standard Restaurant Equipment Company, Family Stores True Value, East Side Market, Best Distributing, Spiffy Ice, Little Red School House, the Co-op Mine in Huntington and AAA Security, among others. They also own a pawn shop, bar and a gambling establishment as well as other business.

As Stacy entered her teenage years, she felt increasingly under scrutiny by the group leaders. Part of the religious teaching of the group is that no church member can reach heaven unless one of his daughters is married to a Kingston leader. As the leadership openly considered which of the young women would become their next wives, Stacy was increasingly nervous about their growing interest in her. And instead of having marriage on her mind, she felt an overwhelming desire to finish high school and go to college. "I'd do everything I could think of to make myself less attractive so those men wouldn't be after me—wear baggy clothes and cut my hair short," she says. The leaders reminded Stacy of her father, whom she had grown to hate. "I couldn't stand the idea of them looking at me. I thought they were stupid and disgusting."

The feelings Stacy had for the leaders became public knowledge after an evening in her grandmother's basement. She and several girlfriends were gathered together with Paul Kingston, the man who is now the prophet of the church. All of his wives were in the basement as well. "Paul began singing along with some old '50s record. It was like an Elvis movie, and all the girls and his wives were swooning as he sang to each one," she says. "He came over to me and got down on one knee, taking my hand and singing along with the record. I threw his hand down and ran out saying how I just couldn't stand it."

Stacy had rejected the future prophet, a man who was believed to be directly related to Jesus. Within the church, Stacy would not be forgiven for that singular rejection.

Inside their isolated world, Stacy and three female cousins had tightly bonded during their years growing up together. The four girls made plans and shared dreams for their future. "Unfortunately, in a group such as the Kingstons, our dreams were not possible for girls to attain without losing our salvation," she says. "We were supposed to be getting direction from God about who to marry, but it never made sense to me that God would make you marry someone you couldn't stand."

One of the four girls, Carla, had dreams of becoming an attorney like her father. At age 16, she was asked to be in the wedding line of another cousin and later dreamed that she was herself marrying the groom. "I remember her saying how sick this made her, and how she hoped the dream wasn't a direction from God," says Stacy. "Her mistake was telling her mother about the dream." Carla's mother decided the dream was indeed "direction," and told the leader of the church who was also the father of the groom. Arrangements were then made for Carla to marry the groom, who by now had two wives. He was, in fact, her first cousin, David O. Kingston. "She and I talked about it and about how she didn't love him," remembers Stacy. "I tried to convince her that the dream was just a coincidence but, to her, God had spoken."

Carla was told she would be able to finish high school and go to college if she would follow the plan God had set for her. She was told she would be taken care of and would soon fall in love with her husband. Then the leader himself talked to her, telling her that marrying his son would be the best path for her. Within weeks, Carla was married. "She told me later that having sex with her husband made her sick," says Stacy. "She had to quit school in the middle of her junior year because she was so sick with her pregnancy. A few years later, she told me I was right; but by then it was too late—she had two little girls and a baby on the way."

Stacy recalls times when Carla and another of David's wives would call each other on the phone when it was the other's turn to have him over. "They laughed that the other one had to have sex with him," she says. "They would call and say, 'Ha, ha' and then hang up."

The friendship between Carla and Stacy faded after Carla was forbidden to see Stacy. "I couldn't visit her anymore because she was being watched and when we'd talk on the phone about meeting somewhere, they always found out," says Stacy. "Now she lives in a one-room basement apartment. By the time she turned 27, she had eight kids."

The third of their group was Carla's sister, Ortella, whose only aspiration was to marry within the church and have children. She married her half-brother as his fourth wife. Stacy lost contact with Ortella and only occasionally hears about her. Last she knew, Ortella had four children.

The last of the four friends had planned for her whole young life to be an architect. "Mona loved to design houses and said she couldn't stand kids, so she thought she should spend her life designing buildings," remembers Stacy. "She held out through one year of college; but when I was going to transfer to the same college, her parents got afraid of my influence on her." So the family made Mona an offer. She could finish college at another school, design her own house and be a first wife. They presented her with a list of unmarried men in the church. She chose one and was soon married. "Now Mona lives in a trailer in the Kingston's mining camp. She didn't get to go back to college," says Stacy. "She's not allowed to see me, and last I heard she had eight children that she doesn't take care of very well."

Losing her close childhood friends has had an impact on Stacy. "I was pissed off about all my cousins getting married. I can't form friendships beyond family members after all of that," says Stacy. "Besides, if you become friends with people, you just have to tell them where you're from. It's a big thing. It kept me from running for office in school."

When Stacy was 22, the church was making its annual rounds of visiting all the group's families to reaffirm their allegiance to the religion. Each year, members are to sign a form stating their loyalty to the group and firm belief in the religion. They must sign a document swearing that when they die, everything they own will go to the church. "Just days before this visit, my mom had been mailed an envelope with home-made porn pictures of one of the leader's wives," says Stacy. "We'd all heard for a long time that this had been going on with a lot of people, but then Mom got the pictures and it was proof." With the family gathered for their yearly signing of forms, Stacy's mother threw the pictures on the table, asking the leaders how this was spiritual. An excuse was made about other people's business. "My brother tore up his form and walked out," says Stacy. "It was the grand finale for us kids."

Stacy finished college and married a loving, protective man much like the imaginary father she once created in her childhood. Together, they are raising twin daughters and a son far removed from the Kingston church. "My friends, my family of origin and I were just unfortunate enough to be born into a cult," she says. "That's all."

Stacy is one of the founding members of Tapestry, along with her mother, Rowenna, Vicky Prunty and Lillian Bowels. She later left Tapestry to concentrate on her marriage, children and career, but she supports Tapestry and helps when time permits. "There is so much deception and intimidation going on in the cults that fear overpowers individuals, and they choose polygamy out of desperation. They need to know that a choice does exist," says Stacy.

The names of Stacy's girlfriends have been changed.

5.

"I cannot live without my life."
—Emily Bronte

LAURA

Perhaps no one else has seen and lived through more of the inner workings and daily lives of as many varied Mormon fundamentalist polygamist groups as Laura Chapman. Based on her firsthand experiences and observations, there is one message above all others that she wants to convey about living in polygamy: incest, statutory rape, physical, sexual and emotional abuse, deprivation of education and forced marriages of young girls are endemic to all of the polygamist communities and not, as some have proclaimed, no worse than in the general monogamous population or isolated to only a few polygamous groups.

Laura is an articulate woman in her early 40s. As is common for young girls in polygamist homes, she was pulled out of public school at age 11. After leaving polygamy, however, she managed to receive her high school equivalency degree and earn a bachelor's degree in sociology and human development with a minor in psychology. Her educational feats are all the more an achievement considering she accomplished them while working part-time and being a single parent to four daughters and a son with special needs.

It is her education combined with her life experiences that makes Laura's perspective unique. "I did my field work for more than 30 years before I got my formal education," she says.

And though Laura has been threatened since leaving her community, she does not shy away from telling her story. "I have no shame attached to things I had no control of as a child, and maybe through my experience, I can help others who have gone through this," she says. Laura admits it has not been easy. "But that's me, always trying to do the impossible, right down to my unruly hair that I could never make stay in those tight braids and waves all the girls had to wear," she laughs.

During her childhood of long, tight braids and dresses that covered all but her face, Laura began questioning the lifestyle her family was living. For a brief period of time, her family, members of the Fundamentalist Church of Jesus Christ of Latter-day Saints (FLDS), was living in Salt Lake instead of in the main settlement community located on the Arizona-Utah border. During this time, she and her siblings were attending public school instead of being home-schooled, as most polygamists outside the tight-knit communities often are. One day in kindergarten, she committed what she calls "the unthinkable" by bringing a little friend home with her from school. A black friend. "I was told afterward never to bring friends home because my father might go to prison," she recalls. "And then I was told not to be friends with 'Negroes' because they are the seed of Cain, and if I married one, it would be 'death on the spot.'"

This doctrine is held by all Mormon fundamentalist polygamists, who refer to statements made by early leaders of the Mormon Church. The historic Mormon teaching that blacks are the descendants of Cain and "cursed" with black skin through that lineage as punishment for pre-mortal sins is traced to Brigham Young, who held the view that those of African decent were inferior to whites. (Bush and Mauss, *Neither White nor Black*, Signature Books, 1984, pp. 40-41) Brigham Young said of blacks, "[A]ny man having one drop of the seed of [Cain] in him cannot hold the priesthood and if no other Prophet ever spake it before I will say it now in the name of Jesus Christ I know it is true and others know it." The belief is also supported in Mormon scripture found in the *Pearl of Great Price* (Moses 7:8 and Abraham 1:20-27).

In 1964, U.S. President Lyndon Johnson signed into law the Civil Rights Act. Intense public criticism of the church's policy followed, and in 1978, the Mormon Church's president, Spencer W. Kimball, announced a revelation from God giving Mormon black males the right to hold the priesthood and allowing them full membership privileges. The abrupt change was a shock to many faithful LDS and caused many mainstream Mormons to convert to Mormon fundamentalist polygamist groups.

For her activism, Laura continues to use the surname that is on her birth certificate. "It was my father's middle name, which he gave me to hide his paternity; so it's not his surname either," she says. "Kind of like how the Kingstons just choose names out of the phone book."

Because of the mixture of arbitrary names given to offspring, genealogies can be difficult. Individuals, however, are clearly aware of family ties due to a belief of royal lineage. "I'm related to just about everyone in Utah who has anything to do with polygamy," Laura laughs. "And if they keep reproducing like they do, I'll eventually be related to about half the state of Utah." Indeed, Laura's pedigree goes back eight generations in Mormon fundamentalist polygamy, reading like a who's who of Utah's own home-grown religions. Her father was arrested in the 1953 raid on the group in Short Creek, now known as the twin cities of Colorado City, Arizona, and Hildale, Utah, where Laura was born and raised. Rulon Allred, murdered (by members of the LeBaron polygamist group) leader of the Allred group, was her great-uncle on her mother's side. Her grandfather was Morris Kunz, who was held in high regard among independent polygamists for refusing to sign an affidavit denouncing polygamy to get out of jail. Laura married into the Barlow family group, while her aunt married into the LeBaron group.

There are an estimated 10,000-15,000 members of the Colorado City and Hildale polygamist communities in which she grew up. Although this group does not intermarry as closely as the Kingston clan does, they do intermarry. According to Laura, one of the leaders tells members that it is all right to marry relatives as close as cousins and uncles to nieces because God will change the blood so that it is not related. Like the Kingstons, they are also producing children with genetic disorders such as Down and Tourette's Syndromes as well as other birth defects. They also deal constantly with certain communicable diseases and illnesses as a result of not inoculating their children. Whooping cough becomes an annual tradition.

Laura describes a world for girls in which there is clearly no semblance of childhood and no innocence. The high prevalence of pedophile behavior dominates the culture, while the victims are forced to revere their abusers. "It would be difficult to pull a girl out of Colorado City who hasn't been sexually assaulted," she claims. "I know girls as young as 12 years old who have been forced to marry their stepfathers."

When Laura was four, one of her stepbrothers tied her to a bedpost and attempted to rape her. "Afterward I was crying. My father told me he would slap me until I stopped crying, which he proceeded to do," she remembers. "My mother made herself busy in the kitchen so she wouldn't have to watch."

Besides the sexual abuse endured by girls, they're also condemned to a life of virtual slavery. "At age ten, I was baking a dozen loaves of bread at a time," she recalls. "By 13, I was cooking meals for our entire family [of 36 people] and sewing clothes."

Beatings by her father and one of his four wives were common occurrences. Laura and her siblings suffered welts over minor infractions. "No mother can protect her own child from the other mothers," Laura explains.

Born the 25th of her father's 31 children, Laura's earliest memories are of molestation and rape by her father when her mother was gone. Later when he moved all four wives and 31 children into one house, she says, "He would enter my room at night. I would wake up to his perverted acts, trembling in fear for hours after he left. That lasted until I was 13." Between the ages of 13 and 15, she was routinely fondled by some of her brothers. "When I confided to my mom what my brothers were doing, we had to go to my father about it," she remembers. "He told my mom he wanted to talk to her alone; when she came out, she said, 'Your father says we have to let (brothers) be who they're going to be.'" Ironically, according to Laura, people in the group are fond of saying that her father is "one of the most Christ-like men they've ever met."

For Laura, there were no options living in a community that demands unquestioning allegiance and obedience to all men. It is a community that preaches, "You can all but kill a child for deliberately disobeying." There were no options when prayer is the only solution to your problems, when you do not know you can call 911, and when your mother is powerless to protect you from beatings inflicted by the other mothers or from sexual assault by your father and brothers.

"I can remember being suicidal as far back as age six but not knowing how to do it," Laura remembers. "So I'd lay on my bed and will my heart to stop beating or to stop my breath." At age 15, she tried to run away after a beating by her mom's sister, who was also a sister-wife.

On her 16th birthday, her father took her for a ride in his Cadillac because it was time for her "Sexuality Lesson." It was a tradition for all her father's daughters and his attempt to legitimize the rape of them that was already ongoing. Driving down the highway at 60 m.p.h., he told her not to tell her mother about the lesson because sister-wives don't tell each other about intimacies. "He told me, 'You are to think of yourself as a sister-wife to your mothers.' My father basically married me emotionally while I had my hand on the door handle debating whether or not to pull it and jump to my death," she remembers. But Laura didn't jump. She survived that night of terror, as she would others.

Her sister, married at 17 to a 70-year-old leader of the church's council, tried to press Laura into an arranged marriage to a man she didn't know. However, she knew a 20-year-old boy from the Barlow group who was a friend of her brother's, so she asked to marry him instead. "I wasn't in love and he wasn't either, but at least we knew each other some," she says, adding with pride, "I became the first girl in the group not to marry a man I was told to marry."

Although she was her husband's first wife, they were married without the benefit of a legal marriage. Laura moved in with his parents among the Barlow group. She remembers they had platitudes to live by: "Women are vessels to be worn out in childbirth," and another, "One child is worth ten of the mother." She would soon experience these sentiments firsthand.

Among the Barlows, Laura saw the same abuses that she experienced in the Colorado City group and in the Allred group where her mother's relatives lived. They were the same abuses she saw her cousins endure in the LeBaron group and with the independents she knew through her grandfather. In the house where she was now living with her in-laws, Laura was silently watching. "I could hear my father-in-law's second wife beating the children," she remembers. "The same wife told me how her husband threw her down the stairs while she was pregnant."

Her father-in-law's second wife soon became plagued with genital herpes on her rectum while the small grandchildren became infected with genital herpes in and on the mouth, suggesting child sexual abuse by the grandfather as the disease is spread only by genital contact. "They actually went to this one doctor that all the Barlows go to even though they don't believe in doctors," Laura relates. "He told the mother to talk to the children about sexual abuse and wanted her and my father-in-law to come in for marriage counseling. That was all that happened."

Laura's husband worked on and off for his father, but they could never make ends meet due to his chronic unemployment. The couple was continually moving in and out of his parents' home while Laura gave birth to five children. "All I had to eat during most pregnancies was toasted bread and canned fruit," she says. "As long as I could be frightened, confused and in poverty, I'd have no way out." Although the Barlows believe that taking birth control is killing your children, Laura made it known to her husband that she just wanted to do right by the five children she already had and didn't want any more. He told her if she used birth control, he wouldn't have anything more to do with her.

Later, Laura confided to her husband the sexual abuse she had suffered from her father and brothers. Instead of outrage, he told her how he, at the age of 19, had molested his 11-year-old sister. "From then on, I knew I couldn't trust him with our daughters," she says. "I began planning my escape and going to the local library to find out how to talk to my children about sexual abuse."

Their tenth anniversary was another clincher for Laura's resolve to leave. He presented her with a ring, and then told her he had to take another wife in order to go to the Celestial Kingdom. She talked him into making their marriage legal, planning for the time that she could demand child support. He agreed and they had a legal ceremony performed on May 9. By July 1, she and her children moved out. Laura says her ex-husband didn't try to contact their children until after he had taken a second wife. "He began co-habiting with a 16-year-old before our divorce was final," she says. Laura could not find an attorney to help her fight her husband's right for visitation with their children. "I've all but sweat blood to give them a different life," she says. "How many parents would want their daughters to go to Colorado City? Don't I have the right to protect my children from that? Their father married an underage girl and lives in a community of organized crime. I should have state and legal assistance behind me."

She describes leaving polygamy and going into the outside world as comparable to taking people from a third world country and setting them down in a large metropolitan city with terrorists after them. "It's harrowing, and there is no one there for you like there is when gang members leave," she says. "Polygamy is about gangs of criminals, too."

In the process of building a life for herself and her children, Laura began getting word from her sisters about other girls still involved in polygamy who were being molested and raped. Laura called the Utah Division of Child and Family Services (DCFS) about one of the girls who had been raped by her father. She then approached the girl and told her that she had already reported the girl's father. "She freaked and told her husband, who is also my 56-year-old former father-in-law," says Laura. Laura's former father-in-law then told Laura that she had her way of dealing with things and they had theirs; he then told his young wife to pack her things. "He said to me, 'You don't know what we've gone through to keep her from state authorities,'" Laura recalls. "Then they drove to Colorado City and across state lines, which is a federal offense. And the Utah DCFS dropped the case."

It is a misdemeanor in the state of Utah for a person who knows about child abuse not to report the crime to authorities. In polygamy, when people report the abuse, they have their lives threatened by the polygamist group. Because of just such threats, Laura and her children went to the YWCA shelter for safety. "They almost didn't let me in because my husband wasn't beating me," she says. "I really didn't feel safe in Utah because I figured no one will take this seriously."

Laura asks rhetorically, "For how many years will the state look the other way while laws are broken by these people? Twelve years ago, after my sister left her polygamous husband and was staying at a different residence, she was abducted on her paper route," she says. "My sister was then held in her room and threatened to be killed in blood atonement. The police said, 'You can't be abducted in your own home.'"

Laura learned about the newly formed group Tapestry around the time that the accusations against the Kingston cult surfaced in the media. When she heard about the bruised and bloodied 15-year-old Mary Ann's claims that she was beaten by her father, John Daniel Kingston, for running away from a marriage to her 32-year-old uncle, David Kingston, Laura became involved. As a representative of Tapestry, she called the Utah DCFS to ask what was being done about the statutory rape and incest accusations against the uncle. "The social worker said they were waiting for charges to be pressed," recalls Laura. "So I said, 'Look, she's a minor in your custody, and you have to be the ones to press charges.' I actually had to tell DCFS how to do their job."

Just after leaving her work with Tapestry in 1999, Laura became involved in helping two girls escape the FLDS church, from which she herself had escaped years earlier.

The two 16-year-olds, Sarah Cook and Kathy Beagly, were frantic to leave before being forced to marry men who they were told were as old as their fathers. The girls told Laura that if they were turned over to state protective services, they would run away. Her answer was, "Then I'll create a new path."

Before embarking on that path, she needed to be able to say she gave protective services a chance. "I called and talked to Ken Patterson [former director of the DCFS] and asked him what to do about girls being forced into marriages," she says. "He told me that before he could act, they would have to be forced to have sex."

Laura then searched for an attorney and, after being turned down by several, finally found one who advised her to cover herself against charges of kidnapping. In order to do that the girls had to draft letters stating that at age 16 they were old enough to know they did not want to live polygamy, did not want to be forced into marriage, wanted to go back to school and that they chose to leave on their own accord. Then Laura found foster parents in her area so that they wouldn't have to cross state lines. After completing a background check on the foster parents, she introduced them to the girls. Late one night, the girls quietly slipped away from their families to meet Laura at a designated spot. Laura drove them to their foster homes.

Sarah met with school counselors and staff who were made aware of her situation and she was taken under the wing of a foster sister to learn the ropes of high school. Under legal advice, her foster parents went to court and became her legal guardians. Sarah has soared and is now attending college in another state, staying on the honor roll and receiving a scholarship.

Kathy did not stay long with her foster parents due to the influence of a sister who connected her back with her family. She returned to the community only to leave once more and reconnect with the foster family, who then helped her with tutoring and getting accepted into college.

"They have to have a caring, responsible family to help them because the outside is so shocking; they're so inept at dealing with it that they aren't ready to be emancipated," says Laura.

Laura left Tapestry to pursue anti-polygamy activism on her own and has also moved from Utah with her children in the hope of beginning a new life. In March of 2002, she and New York University Law Professor Donna Sullivan addressed a women's conference at the United Nations concerning the human rights violations in polygamy. It was the pinnacle of her activism. As for those who abused her, she doesn't hesitate, "My best revenge is to live a healthy life."

6.

*[A] successful polygamous wife must regard her husband
with indifference, and with no other feeling
than that of reverence, for love we regard as a false
sentiment; a feeling which should have no
existence in polygamy.*
                           —Zina D. Jacobs Smith Young, 1869

CARMEN

As the only girl born to parents newly converted to Mormonism, Carmen
Thompson's earliest memories are marked by continuous pressure to
live the perfect Mormon girl ideal and ultimately reach the Celestial
Kingdom. "All my concerns revolved around pleasing my parents," she
remembers. "And once my father became a member of the bishopric
there was even more pressure."

During the late 1960s, Carmen's family lived in Illinois, where
Carmen, who was in elementary school, was caught in the effort to ra-
cially integrate schools by busing children. "I was one of five white students in the school at a time when my religion withheld the priesthood
from blacks," she says. "Blacks weren't allowed in our temples, and my
parents feared for my future because there was potential for me to marry
a black."

To ensure that their daughter had every opportunity to marry a white
Mormon male, the family moved to Utah when Carmen was 11. At age
16, Carmen struggled with the priesthood issue in the same way many
others did, asking, "If God is the same today, yesterday and forever, then
this policy change is wrong. And if this is wrong to change, the same is
true for the polygamy issue."

Other lessons Carmen had absorbed played through her mind like a broken record. "My history teacher in Illinois taught us how the Mormons established the practice of polygamy while they were headquartered in Nauvoo. It was the first I knew of it, and my father reinforced that in later discussions," she says. "Then in Utah, in Sunday School class, I learned that since there are more women than men [polygamy was required for all of them] to make it to the Celestial Kingdom. I did the math and saw that polygamy was my future."

After enduring a long crisis of faith, she was then faced with leaving home for the first time as a young adult. "I went to college where I had more freedom than I knew what to do with," she says. "By age 18, I had become pregnant; so I moved back home to have my son and to deal with my guilt for having a child out of wedlock."

After her son was born, Carmen enrolled in LDS (Latter-day Saint) Business College in Salt Lake, taking classes in court reporting. "I met a lot of people who felt the same way I did about the church. Some were fundamentalists and some were quasi-fundamentalist," she says. "Then I met a student named Stacy who took me under her wing and introduced me to polygamy."

Carmen was soon introduced to Stacy's brother, who then told Carmen he had had a revelation that she would marry him. "He was from mainstream Mormonism like me, and he knew all the theology and history," she says. "After knowing him for three days, I married him as his sixth wife. I didn't love him, but I felt he was sent to me by God."

Just a year before their marriage, Carmen's new husband had been stealing ammunition from the Army base in Tooele, Utah. Caught in a sting operation, he lost his job as a police officer and his access to the base. Unknown to authorities, however, he had buried much of his stolen ammunition in the Utah desert awaiting Armageddon. "I felt very safe knowing that it was there for our eventual protection," says Carmen. "The ammunition had been intended to sell to Iran. He had planned to make millions on the deal."

The punishment for his theft was a year of probation and a promise that he would have only one wife. "He had the six of us, but we had to maintain the appearance of him only having one wife; so I was chosen to go with him to California," she says.

"We were there on a ranch working, and then the first wife and her kids came out for a visit. She was ovulating and wanted to conceive, so I watched the kids while he and she were in the bedroom." That first night, in her private torment over her husband being in bed with his first wife, Carmen lay awake until 4 a.m. praying to fall asleep. "When I woke up knowing that I'd at last fallen asleep, I took it as a sign that living polygamy was what I was supposed to do."

Within a few days, Carmen's husband and the first wife were embroiled in a heated argument that had the woman packing to go back to Utah. "She told me that I needed to get away from him, and then she said, 'He raped our daughter.'" Carmen confronted him, but he denied it, saying the woman believed it of every man because her father had molested her. "I didn't want to believe it, so I didn't," says Carmen. His continuous religious rhetoric only increased his lofty position in her mind. "He was getting revelations from God, and I just thought he was so holy and spiritual."

After 18 months in California, the two returned to Utah to join the other wives and children. Carmen was pregnant with her third child, having given birth to her second while in California. "We moved into a house with his sister Stacy and another one of the wives," she says. "I then became the caregiver for my children and the children of all the other wives. There were 12 kids under school age."

Another wife was soon added to the family; now with seven women, their husband began a schedule of one wife per night of the week. "We didn't see much of him beyond our night and our religious gatherings." As the years went by, two wives would leave, one to join another fundamentalist religion in Oregon. Carmen's husband refused to support the women and their children, telling them that they had to learn to be financially independent. Each of them endured their own extremes of poverty and homelessness. "At times, my children and I lived in our car. We fished and went 'dumpster diving,'" says Carmen. "My mother was in total denial about my life, and my father would only say that I had to do whatever it took to get to the Celestial Kingdom."

One life crisis came after another. The day after Carmen delivered her fifth child, her father died and her husband took another much younger wife. The combination was more than she could handle. She sunk into despair, unable to get off the couch day after day. "For the first time, I felt alone, depressed and oppressed. My mother forced me to seek therapy where I was encouraged to find something I loved and do it," she says. "Then one of my sister-wives talked me into taking some comedy classes because I was always the funny one who turned to jokes to deal with stress."

She had no money to pay for the course, but she was able to talk the instructor into letting her take classes and defer the payments. After two weeks, the instructor asked her to do a stand-up show for five minutes. "From there I did stand up every week doing material on polygamy," she says. "Before I knew it, I was making money three nights a week and eventually going on tour in nine western states."

Carmen's new vocation offered her much needed money to support her children, but she found something more. "I found a life out there in the world and chances to make my own decisions." She was growing in unexpected ways. Her new independence, however, was putting a strain on her relationship with her husband. "Every time I came home from three weeks gone, I was stronger. The stronger I got, the more physically violent he got with me," she says. "After six years in stand-up comedy, I was realizing I had to get out of polygamy."

In a clandestine plan to leave the family at some future date, she had been stashing money and putting clothes in the trunk of her car little by little so no one would notice. "I got enough together for 90 days and then, as luck would have it, I got home one evening and found the police in the yard. My husband had threatened to kill my son, so my son had called the police. When I walked up to him, he threatened to kill me in front of them," she says. "They arrested him on the spot, so I knew I'd have a 12-hour start on him before they let him out."

As she was summoning up her courage to make the break, she had one last conversation with the newest sister-wife. "I asked her just when it was that our husband had married his own sister. I said it in jest only because he had been hanging around Stacy so much," remembers Carmen. "My sister-wife said, 'Oh, I'm so glad you know.' So I played along to get more information and found out that he and his sister had been married for six months." That conversation gave Carmen the last push she needed. "I packed up the kids and started driving."

The homeless shelter for families was full, but she was told to call at 10 a.m. each day to keep her name on the list. "Then they told me they wouldn't allow my older two boys in the family shelter because they were older than nine years old. They would have to go to the men's shelter," she says. "So I opted to stay in the car and soon found out that no one would rent to a single woman with five children."

Though she hadn't been to the Mormon Church for some time, Carmen decided to reach out to the faith of her childhood and ask for help. "The bishop said he couldn't help me and told me to go back to my husband," she says. "I explained my situation and he said it didn't matter and that my husband needed to support me." In desperation, Carmen contacted a local TV station which found her story compelling enough for a few minutes of air time, leading a viewer to offer a small trailer as shelter.

Once moved into their tiny home, the new family was approached by Mormon missionaries who were out proselytizing in the area. "I asked about having my kids baptized in the LDS church, and they told me I needed to contact my bishop for permission since we'd come out of polygamy," she says. "Then their mission president told me the sins of the mother were on my children, and they couldn't be baptized until they were adults since at any time I could still lead them astray."

With an address and the children enrolled in school, it didn't take long for Carmen's estranged husband to find her and take her to court to fight for custody of the children. "I fought him for a year without an attorney and with a judge who told me that if I made polygamy a reason for not letting my kids be with their father, he'd side against me," she says. "I won only because my husband failed to show up for the last hearing."

With a modicum of peace and stability, Carmen continued to feel a strong desire to talk to other women who would understand what she had been through for the last 15 years, so she turned to the Internet. "The problem was that all the sites having to do with polygamy were run by men," she says. "Then I found Steve Butt on-line. He talked to me for several months before he'd allow me to talk to his wives."

A self-styled polygamous Christian minister, Butt leads The Patriarchal Christian Fellowship of God's Free Men and Women through his Broken Shackles Ministry. He changes locations periodically and was last known to be in Texas. The church claims nearly 14,000 members nationally and they maintain their affiliation with Butt's polygamous church via the Internet, where he found his third and fourth wives. Other Christian fundamentalist polygamists have broken off from Butt and continue their own Internet recruitment.

Zealous proselytizers, Butt and his wives introduced Carmen via the Internet to a Christian couple who were searching for another wife to join their union. "I still believed in polygamy. I thought it could be lived if it was lived right, and that maybe the problem was the Mormon theology," she explains. "After a few months of e-mails and phone calls they asked me to marry him, sold everything they owned and moved to Utah sight unseen. We had our own ceremony five days after they arrived and declared ourselves married."

But the new union was doomed from the start. "That woman went through hell having to share her husband of 15 years," says Carmen. "Her health dwindled and she got emotionally and verbally abusive with me." Within seven months, Carmen knew the marriage and polygamy itself could never work happily.

Because the Butts were relocating their church headquarters from Maine to Utah in order to enjoy Utah's lack of prosecution against polygamists, they decided that they should move in temporarily with Carmen and her husband and sister-wife in Salt Lake City. "They were with us for three months, and I saw the unhappiness and the crying wives," says Carmen. "It's like running into a brick wall, and then you finally realize it's the dynamics of polygamy itself that sets up all the abuse."

By the time the Butts moved on to their own temporary place in Salt Lake (eventually settling in Circleville, Utah), Carmen was becoming increasingly angry with herself for putting herself and her children through another polygamous relationship. Then, just before Christmas, her husband and his first wife turned the heat off in her portion of the house even though she had just brought a child home from the hospital. "I packed up my kids and this time a relative took us in while I finished school."

As Carmen was reclaiming her life, she met and married Michael, a monogamous man who convinced her to pick up the phone and call the new group Tapestry Against Polygamy.

Carmen made the call, and for an interim period she served the organization as its Executive Director. She eventually left to pursue other career ambitions and because she was getting burned out. "I was close to breaking. I had a 24-hour hot line for polygamist women in my bedroom and death threats in my mail and on my voice mail."

During her time serving with Tapestry, her children closely observed her speaking out and standing up for herself. "Watching me do that helped them talk about their own experiences. One day my second son told me something he'd been keeping inside for a long time," says Carmen. "He told me that his father had molested [sodomized] him."

Though happily married at last, Carmen and her children continue to struggle with the scars and residue left by polygamy. One son is presently living on the streets as a runaway. "He has that polygamy mindset of not respecting laws and being subject only to himself," says Carmen. "He's out there self-medicating on drugs." She suspects that some, if not all, of her other children were also abused by her first husband.

Not long after her mother passed away, the family moved from Utah to Pennsylvania in an effort to put distance between themselves and the painful memories of living in polygamy.

7

Never can polygamy cease to be
anything but a series of cruel stings.
—Eliza Ann Young, 19th wife of
Brigham Young, 1887

ALLISON

With the passage of time, Allison Ryan now has a certain perspective on her personal nightmare of having been married at the age of 16 to the media-hungry polygamist Tom Green. But there was a time when she was tormented by years of guilt. "It was what he made me do sexually. I just couldn't believe I did it."

The guilt became so overwhelming that Allison eventually attempted suicide. "I couldn't live with it, that I'd done what he wanted me to do with him," she says. "It's horrible to be treated that way."

Before her encounter with Green, Allison had been raped at age 11 while living in North Carolina. "Being raised LDS, I thought I was dirty now," she says. "Guys at school would grab my breasts, and that just added to my becoming very vulnerable to a predator."

Just as Allison was celebrating her 16th birthday in 1989, her parents moved their family into a trailer court in Sandy, Utah, in an effort to be closer to the Mormon Church. Anxious to make new friends, the Ryan sisters soon discovered the large Green family living next to them. "They had 20 people in a single-wide trailer," she says. "I became friends with his kids that summer; and when Tom and his four wives went to AmWay conventions, they would have me baby-sit, even though they had kids my age."

The baby-sitting became more and more regular as Green's four wives took an interest in Allison—an interest that was instigated by Green. "One time when my little sister and I came to baby-sit, Tom turned to his 16-year-old stepson and said, 'Either you marry them or I will,'" Allison remembers.

Suffering with untreated depression and painfully self-conscious of her weight gain, Allison began Alta High School as the friendless, unlovable new kid in town. Her solution was simply to drop out of school. "My mom told me to get a job, but I still ended up having a lot of free time," she says. "So I spent it with the only other kids around, the Green kids."

One evening, Green asked Allison on a date. "He took me to Park City and talked about sex while rubbing my leg. He told me he wanted me as a wife," she says. "I had such low self-esteem that I thought this was the best I could get and told myself it would probably be good for me." After their date, the Greens had Allison move in with them, an arrangement that her parents agreed to since Allison was not getting along with her mother at the time. "Tom was controlling and intimidating. He treated me like one of his kids, but he was mean to his stepkids," she says. "LeeAnn [his stepdaughter] would go cry out back and tell me that Tom was molesting her." With Allison in their trailer, Green's four wives began pressuring her, telling her they wanted her to marry Tom and be part of their family.

Allison's mother knew Green wanted to marry her daughter, and according to Allison, she went to the Mormon bishop and asked his advice. "She said he told her to support the decision or I might end up a runaway." After living in the Green trailer for two months as one of the kids, Allison was on her way to becoming one of the wives. "To understand how it happened to me, you would have to know about my mother," she says. "She was married to my father at age 16. He went along with everything she wanted, and she wanted to get rid of us girls as soon as possible [to be free of child-rearing duties]."

Indeed, Green's 16-year-old stepson Jim was dating Allison's 12-year-old sister, Andrea. With one wedding on the burner, their mother then granted permission for Andrea to marry Jim at the same time that Allison married Green. "Andrea was crying that day. We both changed our minds, but my mom didn't stop it or announce that we didn't want to go through with it because Tom intimidated her," says Allison. "I remember that day in the trailer park clubhouse getting married just two minutes after he married his own stepdaughter, LeeAnn. Kids were looking in through the windows and I wore a 'polyg' dress that LeeAnn's mother made." Allison became Green's sixth wife.

Twelve-year-old Andrea's "marriage" ended within two weeks. The couple had moved in with Andrea's and Allison's parents, who soon kicked Jim out for being lazy. Allison's mother maintains that Andrea's marriage wasn't a "serious marriage." "Tom said it was just something polygamists do among themselves and we played along with it," she says. "I admit I was intimidated by him. It was a sickening time of our lives that I wish had never happened, and I'll always feel a lot of guilt."

After the wedding, Green drove Allison to Las Vegas for their honeymoon. "He got a hotel room where we got drunk and had sex," she says. "It was humiliating. I felt dirty."

Back in Utah, Green began the business that his wives continue to operate today. "He started his magazine sales and made all of us go door to door and do telemarketing," she says. "He filtered [laundered] money through a friend of his under an assumed name." This enabled the family to continue receiving public assistance, part of Green's delight in "bleeding the beast," or working to bring down the government.

The family continued to live in the single-wide trailer in Sandy. "We all just slept wherever—on the couch, on the floor, on top of clothes. I never saw any home schooling or scripture reading like they try to show people on TV," she remembers. "The wives fought all the time, and the fridge was locked so Tom and the wives could eat the good food. He got food out of the dumpster at an Albertson's for the kids to eat."

Within weeks, Green decided to take his two newest brides to another trailer he had in Elko, Nevada. One of the other wives and a friend were there selling magazines, and he wanted to bring them back to Utah. "When we arrived, we found the friend really sick, near death. But he wouldn't take her to the hospital," says Allison. "I finally convinced him she would die, so he took her. I thought it could be me dying and he wouldn't care." With Green gone to the hospital, Allison called her mother to drive out to get her. When her mother arrived, Allison jumped out a window of the trailer and fled. She had been married for six weeks.

"After I left, I wrote a letter to him saying I loved the wives and kids, but I hated the living conditions," she says. "What I didn't write was how evil he is and how he terrified me." Green still keeps Allison's letter, using her omissions to lay claim that she was happy in his family.

Allison has now found happiness with a new husband with whom she has three young children. She obtained a high school equivalency diploma. "It's taken many years to get where I am, but I'll never be entirely over it," she says.

After ten total marriages, Green has remained married to five young women for more than ten years. At the time of their marriages, his wives ranged from ages 13 to 16 and two were stepdaughters. Though the five wives are now no longer prepubescent or teenagers, they remain in a childish state, forever dressed in little girl frilly frocks and pinafores, white socks and long hair in curls and bows.

As of February 2002, Green has fathered 30 children.

Green loves to be in the national press. Tapestry sent tapes of Green's media appearances to the County Prosecutor, David Leavitt, which led to charges being brought against him. He was convicted of four counts of bigamy and one charge of criminal nonsupport on August 23, 2001. The sentence was five years in prison. Green and his attorney successfully won a battle against his having to undergo a psychosexual evaluation to determine whether he is a pedophile. On August 28, 2002, Green was sentenced to the minimum sentence of five years to life in prison for the first degree felony conviction of child rape for having sex with a "wife" when she was 13.

On the last day of Green's bigamy and nonsupport trial, Allison stood in a packed courtroom and faced Green for the first time since she fled from him that night in Elko 13 years ago. Now, at age 28, she was finally seeing him in a vulnerable position. During cross-examination, prosecutor David Leavitt identified Green's numerous wives and called Allison to the bar. "I looked him straight in the eye," she says with triumph.

8.

JANICE

According to family stories, the matriarchal line in Janice Hepper's family, beginning with her great-grandmother, has been locked in a cycle of self-destruction through addiction to abusive relationships. Like dominoes crashing one after the other, each woman before her had married and eventually divorced alcoholic men. Janice's personal choices in life were different in that her addictions were religious. Added to such destructive family patterns, the trauma of her brutal upbringing remains a persistent echo. "My life was filled with emotional and verbal abuse and no sense of self," Janice says of her San Francisco childhood. "There were no boundaries; and, as a child, the criticism I received from my parents tore into the fabric of my being."

When she was 14 years old, Janice's older brother began a friendship with several Mormon kids at school. It wasn't long before the Mormon boys were proselytizing to him and he, in turn, would share Mormon doctrine with Janice. "He'd come home and we'd talk about what he was learning. It stimulated me intellectually," she remembers. "I soon met the missionaries, and within a month I was baptized into the LDS Church."

At the same time that she was immersing herself in Mormon culture, she was also becoming a sexually active teen. By the age of 19, Janice was a pregnant bride. In 1963, her son was born and her short marriage was ending.

As a single mother without a car, Janice was in need of rides to the Mormon Church as well as a baby-sitter while she worked. She found both in a young couple who were associated with a group of friends known as the "Seven French Missionaries."

In 1958, a number of Mormon missionaries in France led by William Tucker, a counselor to the president of the Mormon mission in France (referred to as the "French mission" and missionaries as "French missionaries" though they were American missionaries in France), were converted to the polygamist group led by the LeBaron brothers, who had been born in the Mormon polygamist hamlet of Colonia Juarez in Chihuahua, Mexico, across the border from El Paso, Texas. (Van Wagoner, p. 203-05)

Tucker had read Mormon fundamentalist polygamist literature prior to his mission and began secretly talking to other missionaries about his beliefs. When one of Tucker's missionary companions, David Shore, returned to Utah after his mission to France, he sent Tucker a copy of Ervil LeBaron's *Priesthood Expounded*. With his considerable influence over other missionaries, Tucker gathered a number of converts from his peers. (Id.)

French mission president Milton Christensen discovered the unorthodox studies and arranged to have Tucker, Stephen M. Silver and J. Bruce Wakeham interviewed by Mormon apostles who were in Europe for the dedication of the London Temple. All other missionaries of the French mission were questioned about their beliefs. Tucker, Silver, Wakeham, Daniel Jordan, Marilyn Lamborn, Neil Poulsen, Loftin N. Harvey, June Abbott and Nancy Fulk were excommunicated and sent home. Harvey Harper, Ron Jarvis and Marlene Wessel returned home on their own without being excommunicated. (Id.)

Seven of the former missionaries, four men and three women, joined LeBaron's new religion. Marilyn Lamborn and Nancy Fulk married Tucker, and June Abbott married Wakeham. Back in the United States, the Seven French Missionaries became vigorous proselytizers for the LeBaron Church of the Firstborn of the Fullness of Times. (Van Wagoner, 1989, p. 204)

As Janice was being taught the doctrines of the church by her attentive new friends, Bruce and June (now calling herself Janay) Wakeham, they also began courting her. "The women do as much courting as the men to try to bring a new wife in," says Janice. "They seemed sophisticated, and he was a very handsome man. I was twenty, very alone, naive and enamored. It was easy for them to court me."

In 1963, at the age of twenty-one, Janice was baptized into the LeBaron group in a San Francisco backyard swimming pool. "It was like a Mormon baptism; and I was confirmed afterward, just like in the Mormon Church," she remembers. "After my confirmation, I was told that the blessing drained the priesthood holder, which implied that there was something special about me and my blessing."

Unlike other Mormon fundamentalist polygamists who claim their line of authority from Lorin C. Woolley, the LeBarons believe that Joseph Smith secretly passed the presidency of the High Priesthood, or the "Right of the Firstborn Sceptre in Israel," to Benjamin F. Johnson in Nauvoo, Illinois, where the Mormons built their first temple. It was there that Johnson was supposed to have passed his authority to his grandson, Alma Dayer LeBaron. Alma told his sons that Johnson appeared to him in the form of an angel and told him of the mission he was to perform and that the "mantle of Joseph Smith" would be passed to his most worthy sons. (Ibid. p. 203)

Alma LeBaron was excommunicated from the Mormon Church, but his sons remained Mormon while growing up in Colonia Juarez, Mexico. The oldest son, Benjamin, claimed that his father had given him the "mantle" and proclaimed himself the "One Mighty and Strong" (from the Mormon *Doctrine and Covenants*) who would reconcile the Mormon Church and all the fundamentalists. At times, Benjamin would let out a roar to prove he was the "Lion of Israel." One day he lay down in a Salt Lake City intersection to do push-ups, holding up traffic for an hour. When the police arrived, he replied, "See, nobody else can do that many. That proves that I'm the 'One Mighty and Strong.'" Benjamin was committed to the Utah State Mental Hospital in 1953. (Van Atta, Dale, "LeBaron Chronicle Echoes Biblical Stories," *Salt Lake Tribune*, 17 June 1977. Van Wagoner, 1989, p. 203)

Back in Mexico, the other brothers were establishing a colony under the direction of Margarito Bautista, who was visiting from the Allred polygamist group. Eventually a power struggle developed between brothers Joel and Ross when Joel LeBaron announced he was the "One Mighty and Strong." Ross broke away and formed his own Church of the First-born. Floren, another brother, followed Joel, and the two converted their mother and other brothers. Joel became the leader and prophet, but it was under the proselytizing directions of another brother, Ervil, and with the help of the Seven French Missionaries that the religion grew to more than five hundred members by 1958. (Van Wagoner, 1989, p. 203)

Soon after Janice's conversion, the Wakehams moved from San Francisco to the LeBaron Mexican colony, leaving Janice lonely, anxious and busying herself to make the move. "I was ready to go to Mexico and marry Bruce," she says. But once in Mexico, Janice discovered that instead of becoming instant family members in the Wakehams' home, she and her son were unwelcome guests. "Bruce," she recalls, "was actually courting another woman in the colony. They both wanted him to marry Janay's best friend Jackie, making me the odd woman out. I felt so alone, isolated and abandoned."

The colony was overcrowded, dirty and impoverished. "A lot of people from Short Creek were there because of the raid a few years earlier. It was really hot in the summer, and we had no refrigeration and no running water," says Janice. "We used wood-burning stoves and lived in small adobe buildings with outhouses."

At the colony, only the Mexican-born LeBarons could own property. "American-born members couldn't own anything and were compelled to work in the States," says Janice.

To escape the continued feeling that she and her son were unwanted in the Wakeham household, Janice spent her time caring for a new friend who had just had a baby while the husband, Paul, was in the United States. One night, Floren LeBaron came to the house looking for Paul. Of the seven LeBaron brothers, Floren was one of three, along with Joel and Ross, who had incorporated their church, The Church of the Firstborn of the Fullness of Times, in Salt Lake City on September 21, 1955.

When Janice first laid eyes on the tall and lanky Floren LeBaron that night in 1963, she thought he was the perfect example of what a country bumpkin might be. "He asked if he could come in and wait for Paul and we ended up talking for hours," she says. And as the hours passed, Janice came to believe that she received a witness of the spirit that he was a good man. "I had a connection with him, and he felt it too."

Within three days, Janice and Floren were married. His first wife, DrewAnn, was working in Las Vegas at the time and would learn about Janice later. "My wedding night was traumatic," says Janice. "I had sex with this man that I didn't love and hardly knew." After the wedding night at the colony, Floren took Janice on a honeymoon to Chihuahua City, Mexico, where her conflicted feelings were heightened by her continued attachment to Bruce. "I wasn't over Bruce, and there I discovered he was honeymooning at the same hotel with his new bride, Jackie," she says. "I had to keep up a front and not let anyone know I was in pain."

After the honeymoon, Floren took Janice to Las Vegas to meet her sister-wife. "Members were working in Vegas and all living in the same house," she explains. "I was sitting in the truck while he went in to announce me to DrewAnn. Then he brought me inside."

Even though Janice had, as she puts it, "taken on the look" of a polygamist, she went to work as a change girl at the Sahara Hotel and Casino in Las Vegas. "I was bouncing between extremes," she says. "At work I got to wear makeup."

Inside the communal house, relationships were growing strained. "Paul would throw dishes on the floor because we were all such slobs, and DrewAnn and I found that we could never be anything but enemies," remembers Janice. "The decision was made that I should go back to Mexico and get more religious training because I couldn't get along."

Back in Mexico, Janice was reunited with her son, and they were put into one of two matching adobe structures. A woman named Vonda was occupying the other structure and the two isolated women soon became close friends. "During the time I was living next to Vonda, I saw a sign of violence in the church," says Janice. "Ervil LeBaron gave us guns and instructions. He said, 'If anyone ever comes around, shoot 'em first and drag 'em inside.'" From other members, she heard other hints and rumors of violence, including mention of several murders that had occurred before her arrival.

The gun instructions may have followed an incident involving Bruce's new wife. One day, the father of Jackie's child from a previous marriage found his way to the colony, looking for his son. The members hid Jackie and the boy inside a chicken coop until the father gave up and left. "An outsider is helpless trying to see a loved one," says Janice. "But I saw something that day. That man confronted Joel LeBaron, the prophet of God, and I could see Joel was scared. The prophet of God was afraid of a regular man."

Other things disturbed her. "Bill Tucker, another of the Seven French Missionaries, was the one who was developing the dogma, the scriptures and commandments; but Joel was taking the credit," she says. "And I saw that Ervil was getting more and more jealous."

Under filthy living conditions, Janice and Vonda were becoming seriously ill. In light of Janice's declining health, Floren and DrewAnn returned from Las Vegas intent on taking Janice to the mountains to see friends. "I was so sick and we were driving on long, bumpy dirt roads. It was miserable," she says. "When we got to the mountains, Floren noticed that my eyes were yellow, but we stayed there with his friends for several days before we went home." By the time they got back to the colony, Janice discovered that Vonda had gone to work in the United States, where she was diagnosed with hepatitis. Janice never received a diagnosis or medical attention. "The members took care of me. I never saw a doctor," she says. "I remember that when I had to relieve myself, they would bury the waste in the ground outside of the colony."

In the meantime, Floren had married a third wife, the daughter of the friends from the mountains. "Ramona made it a little easier for DrewAnn and me to get along," Janice remembers. Ramona became the outsider. "Then we moved to Baja, California, next door to another member and his wives; but in less than a year from when we married, I had enough of being with a man I couldn't love."

The Wakehams, including the second wife, had come up from the colony to work in Buena Park, California. "They were still my dearest friends, almost like parent figures to me; so I stayed with them. Then, I don't know how it happened, but I ended up marrying him as his third wife," says Janice. "One night he was making love to me and his first wife got up for a drink. She heard us and gasped, so he put her in bed with us and made love to us at the same time by alternating between us."

This sexual encounter devastated Janice. She spent the day cowering in a corner with a blanket over her head, weeping. "Something in me was screaming. I was traumatized and violated," she says. "It damaged me in ways I still don't know. Because of that, I left the marriage and I left the church too." Janice had been a member of LeBaron's religion for a total of one and a half years.

From there she found her own apartment and began trying to forget her brief but total entanglement with the LeBarons. "It was hell integrating into society," says Janice. "You hide a piece of yourself. You can't tell co-workers about your life."

As Janice stumbled through the next decades of her life, she would walk into grocery stores and see newspapers with the LeBaron members in the headlines. "I would read those names and say to myself, 'It could have been me in the paper.'"

What Janice and the rest of the nation were reading resulted from another power struggle between the LeBaron brothers. Joel had thrown Ervil out of the church and, in August of 1972, Joel was shot to death in what Ross said, "came down to a fight over the birthright, just like in the Bible." (Van Atta, Dale, "LeBaron Chronicle Echoes Biblical Stories," *Salt Lake Tribune*, 17 June 1977, Van Wagoner, 1989, pp. 203-206)

Then, in 1975, five more people were killed. Later, Ervil's "Lambs of God" led a night raid on Los Molinos, Mexico, bombing homes and gunning down residents. Two people were killed and 15 were wounded in the community founded by Joel several years earlier.

Several more of Ervil's "enemies" disappeared and were presumed to have been killed, including Robert Simmons, a Grantsville, Utah, polygamist. Ervil then ordered the death of his unbelieving daughter, Rebecca LeBaron. At the same time, defector Dean Vest was shot to death in National City, California, by one of Ervil's plural wives, Vonda White, Janice's dear friend and former neighbor. Vonda was found guilty and received a life sentence in 1979.

Ervil's chief rival was Rulon C. Allred, leader of the Salt Lake Mormon fundamentalist polygamist group known as the Apostolic United Brethren. Ervil announced to his flock that Allred's murder should be carried out by the group's two prettiest women. Two women were chosen after nominations had been taken. (Bradlee, Ben Jr. and Dale Van Atta, *Prophet of Blood—The Untold Story of Ervil LeBaron and the Lambs of God*, New York: G.P. Putnam's Sons, 1981; Van Wagoner, 1989, pp. 205-206)

On May 10, 1977, the 71-year-old Allred was working at his naturopathic office in Murray, Utah, when Ramona Marston and Rena Chynoweth entered the office through the busy waiting room and shot several bullets into Allred, killing him instantly.

Ervil LeBaron was eventually tried in a U.S. court in 1980 and died of a massive heart attack in his cell at the Utah State Prison. Before his death, he compiled a "hit list" of people who he felt deserved "blood atonement," inscribed in his "Book of New Covenants." Several individuals were killed on his behalf, including Daniel Jordan, one of the Seven French Missionaries. In June 1988, the Lambs of God shot to death Duane Chynoweth and his daughter Jennifer, in Houston, Texas. Simultaneously, Chynoweth's brother Mark, a son-in-law of Ervil, was murdered ten miles away, while 300 miles away, Eddie Marston, one of Ervil's stepsons, was also murdered. (Ibid, pp. 205-208)

The LeBaron group continues to grow today in the same Mexican colonies as well as in Utah and Southern California. They still believe in blood atonement killings and have adopted a doctrine of incestuous marriage between fathers and daughters and between siblings, pointing to God and Mary's conception of Jesus as well as the biblical story of Adam and Eve's offspring multiplying and replenishing the earth.

Janice's experience continued to impact her life to such a degree that she again found herself in a damaging relationship, this one lasting six years and producing a daughter who is now an adult. She also has had to deal with the suicide of her 14-year-old son. Today, at 58, she is single and has completed a bachelor's degree in social work. She is living temporarily, free of charge, in one bedroom. She continues to struggle with the pieces of her life. She has returned to the Mormon Church, believing polygamy will be lived correctly someday. "Polygamy was—is—a part of my life," she says.

9.

*I suppose I could have walked out of the
apartment and away from it all, but I didn't.
It simply never occurred to me.*
—Patty Hearst

CORA

Cora Fischer was the last daughter in a family of four girls born to staunch Mormon parents determined to live the gospel as found in the "revealed" scriptures, or at least to make sure their daughters did. Searching for others who were like-minded, they began attending meetings held by Mormon polygamist fundamentalists of the LeBaron group who gathered weekly in Salt Lake to recruit mainstream Mormons into their ranks. The family was easily drawn in and soon moved to the LeBaron's colony in Mexico. Two years later, they left after a dispute over a healing blessing.

Back in Salt Lake, Cora's parents worried that their extroverted daughter was becoming "too wild." They decided she would grow up more righteously if she were sent to live in the Mormon fundamentalist polygamist twin cities of Colorado City, Arizona, and Hildale, Utah, formerly Short Creek, where every resident, including the local police, is a member of the Fundamentalist Church of Jesus Christ of Latter-day Saints (FLDS).

Once in Colorado City, 12-year-old Cora found herself living with a woman who boarded other young girls sent by their families from Salt Lake. She remembers two sisters, who lived in the house with her briefly, leaving after marrying the same man as plural wives. One of them was nine years old.

All the women and girls in this religion wear long-sleeved, ankle-length dresses over leggings so that they are completely covered. Women wear their hair in buns and girls wear long braids with waves in front. They shun makeup and the color red, as it is believed to be the color reserved for Jesus when he returns to earth.

By age 14, Cora was asked to be the second wife of a 23-year-old man who gave her occasional rides to see her parents in Salt Lake. "When I left Salt Lake, I felt abandoned by my parents. Then it would be just me and Robert in the car and he'd put his arm around me. Pretty soon we went to the council for permission to marry," she says. "I wore a blue homemade dress at my wedding and his wife and baby were there."

Cora's sister-wife, Abby, was older than her husband by three years and less than happy about her husband's new, very young wife. "He'd been told by the council to hold back his feelings for me because of the situation," says Cora. "So he slept with her two nights and then just one night with me." In addition, Abby demanded that Cora's bedroom door remain open.

Already mother to an infant, Abby was again pregnant. When the baby girl was born, she turned her over to Cora. "I basically adopted Renee. She was like my own." Within nine months of her marriage, Cora became pregnant herself.

Under the roof of a newly built home in Colorado City, Cora became "Mom" to all the children, while "mama Abby" worked full time. "I loved all her kids," says Cora. "I diapered, potty trained and loved them. I made all their school clothes and was there for them." Abby would eventually have nine children by Robert. Cora would have eight, but was forced to live outside the family home during her pregnancies.

"Abby couldn't stand to see me pregnant, so I'd live outside of town and walk to the house every day after she left," Cora remembers. "I was 15 during my first pregnancy and so scared all alone at night."

Cora's domestic and nurturing skills never softened her sister-wife's feelings for her. "Abby told me that the only reason she let me come into the family was to be the servant," she says. "And it was the case because I did it all." In addition, Abby would take every opportunity to treat Cora cruelly. "If she wanted me to clean a drawer, she would dump it on the floor before she went to work," she remembers. In one particular incident, Robert joined Abby in inflicting tremendous emotional pain on Cora. On a night when it was Abby's turn to sleep with Robert, Cora got out of the shower and saw what appeared to be Robert in her bed. "I was so excited to get another night," she says. "But when I pulled back the covers, there were socks piled underneath to look like a person's form." As the door to Abby's room shut, Cora could hear them both laughing. She cried herself to sleep that night.

In the years that followed, Abby began getting sick. Healing blessings and prayers failed her. Robert took her to alternative healers, traveled to Mexico to a health center and tried special diets. Nothing helped, so he finally went against the council and took her to a doctor. Her diagnosis was a cancerous brain tumor requiring chemotherapy. It was Cora who nursed Abby around the clock through the remaining years of her life. Because a pregnancy would aggravate her fragile medical condition, the doctor ordered Abby not to have any more children. But polygamist women are to have a child per year so she had three more babies. The last one she delivered while dying—unconscious, without knowing she had given birth.

With Abby gone, Cora was able to turn her attention to other problems in the family. She was becoming increasingly upset about the way

Robert disciplined the children. "He would hold the kids under water in the bathtub until they passed out," she says, "One time he held the inside of Renee's [Abby's daughter] arm against a light bulb until her skin melted."

And there was something else about Robert's behavior. To teach the girls about sexuality he would demonstrate for them on himself where to touch and what to do to a man. Then one day he told Cora to talk to Renee about starting her period. "I asked her if she had started, and she cried and cried saying she was bleeding because her dad had stuck his finger up her," says Cora. "I went to the council and told them what he did, but they wouldn't do anything. So I started sleeping with the girls and locking my door at night."

Eventually, a family member outside of the group visited and became curious about the sleeping arrangements. The relative discovered the abuse and threatened to expose the entire community unless something was done. When Cora told the council what was about to happen, they and the town police decided Robert was expendable. They reported him to state authorities. He was tried and served three years in prison.

But it was Cora who paid within the community. Generally, the church provides for its members who are in need from the United Effort Plan (UEP), which is based on the early Mormon Church's United Order, but Cora never saw any provisions. "I became the plague for turning Robert in," she says. "Here I was with all these children, and they wouldn't give me any help or food from the UEP." She would awaken in the morning to find garbage dumped in her yard or rotten eggs thrown at the house. No one in town would speak to her.

A month after Robert went to prison, she was told Abby's children would be taken from her. "I went to church with them that last Sunday, leaving my own children at home. I sat in the middle of Abby's children with my arms stretched out to hold them all," she remembers. "I cried and cried, and they cried; and I kept reassuring them that I loved them and was sorry I had to let them go."

The children were sent to live with their uncle, who then married 15-year-old Renee. "She's had eight children by him last I heard," says Cora. "Their uncle turned them all against me. None of them have ever spoken to me since he took them."

Cora and her own children continued to struggle while living in the house. "I kept going to the council and asking for help," she says. "So they came up with three names of men for me to pray about as the right one to marry." One of the names was a man whose parents had been close to her parents, so she chose him.

Within two weeks, she and her second husband, Daniel, were married. At age 28, Cora became the third sister-wife in a new family. The first wife, Sara, was so unhappy with having Cora as a sister-wife that she didn't attend the wedding. In this marriage, Cora was to see the second wife live as the servant that she had been in her first marriage. "Some women are afforded autonomy in polygamy, but it's at the expense of other women having to live in complete servitude," says Cora. "And not a single woman I've ever known is happy even though they all say they are. And believe me, a lot of them confided in me."

Cora and her children continued to stay in the family house, but Daniel wasn't even providing them with basic necessities. There was no heat, and they spent the winter freezing.

Though Daniel would spend only one night a week with her, within nine months she was pregnant. "As soon as I got pregnant, he didn't want to deal with me," she says. So, after the birth of her baby, she drove to Salt Lake to stay with a friend and get a job. "I was working, paying my tithing and going back down to Colorado City for church every Sunday and singing in the choir."

Daniel would visit her sporadically and again she became pregnant. Then, one weekend when she and the children came back to Colorado City to attend church, she was faced by men with guns inside her house. They told her that the council was taking the house since she had brought shame on the community with her allegations of sexual abuse against Robert.

This incident caused a split in the community at large. Other members began to worry that their property could also be seized, resulting in factions that divided the church into two separate "wards" led by separate members of the council, who also split over the issue.

Cora then received another bombshell when one of her daughters and a daughter from Daniel's first wife told her that he was molesting them. She had learned not to deal with council leaders about such matters, so this time she went to a family friend. Daniel denied the accusations and the matter was dropped.

After the property seizure, Daniel relocated Cora and her ten children outside of Colorado City. The first stop was a farm 15 miles from their nearest neighbor. She and the children lived without electricity, heat or running water and slept on the floor around a butane heater. They also found themselves in Cedar City, Utah, and San Antonio, Texas. He later moved them to a one-bedroom shanty with no windows in tiny Tropic, Utah. Again they survived with no source of heat except a pot-belly stove. "In every little place, I'd haul out my sewing machine and art supplies," says Cora. "I made every place as beautiful as I could, sewing curtains and doing my art."

After months of moving from one poverty-stricken existence to another, her two oldest teenaged boys decided to find work in Arizona. In the midst of this, Cora found herself pregnant once more and delivered her eleventh child. Soon after, Daniel made it known that he had his eye on one of Cora's daughters for a wife. When the daughter wasn't interested, he became enraged and left immediately.

Having long desired more education, Cora decided to earn her high school equivalency degree in Tropic. Her plan was derailed when Daniel visited and she became pregnant with her twelfth child. Her new friends from the Tropic Christian Church had been trying to help her and, with the news of the latest pregnancy, told her they would get her moved where Daniel couldn't find her.

On her own, she found herself lost in the world and going from place to place searching for a home. At one point, she and the children moved to St. George, Utah. "We lived in a motel where I earned money by cleaning," she says. "We had to keep the little ones quiet in the room so no one would know how many of us were there. I would find food in dumpsters for us to eat." One day, Cora came back from cleaning to find her third oldest son packing. He told her he didn't want to eat the food the younger kids needed. He was 15 years old and had decided to hitchhike to Phoenix and find a job with his brothers. "I hugged him and we both cried," she says. "I was so scared for him to go at such a young age."

Still pregnant, Cora and the nine remaining children moved to Las Vegas and lived in her truck. "I'd sleep in the cab on the seat and the children slept in the camper," she remembers. "We'd drive to the park at night, and I'd comb their hair at a park bench every morning." After working for several weeks as a change girl at the Four Queens, Cora was finally able to rent a small apartment.

Just before her baby was due, one of the children called Daniel without her knowing. He arrived in time for the birth. "He hid in the closet while I had the baby in my bed," she says. "A midwife was attending me, and he was worried he would be caught as a polygamist."

After the birth of the baby, Daniel wouldn't let Cora stay in Las Vegas. He moved her and the children to Phoenix into a tiny trailer with no air conditioning. Feeling she needed to make some kind of life for herself, Cora enrolled in graphic design school. Then, just two months before she was scheduled to finish her classes, Daniel returned and moved her back to Las Vegas.

Through the latest rounds of moving, Cora filled her spare moments in a private world of escape, painting the scenes of a fabulous fairyland story she was creating in her mind. Daniel would move her three more times in Las Vegas while he gambled away the rent money. With rental options running out, he moved her back near Colorado City, next to the group's air strip. Again she found herself in a shack with no running water. This one had no door or glass in the windows. "I was always starting over with nothing," she says. "But I painted the walls, made curtains and got some glass for the windows." The only "neighbors" were the comings and goings at the air strip, which included middle of the night helicopter landings and a car that would drive up to meet it.

When Daniel would come to visit now, he was emotionally abusive with Cora, telling her she was crazy and that Sara, his first wife, meant everything to him. Cora felt she couldn't take any more from him and told Daniel that she was getting the council to release her from their marriage.

On learning this, a young man who had been a friend of her eldest son asked her to marry him. Mark was not a member of the religion, and Cora told him he would have to join if he wanted to marry her. "I was still so brainwashed," she says. "I still believed in playing by their rules as the only way to heaven." Mark joined and in two weeks they were married by the council. He was 23 and she was in her 40s. "I wasn't in love with him, but I was reacting to having someone love me," she explains. "I was really happy."

But Cora's happiness was short-lived. While she and Mark enjoyed a weekend alone, Daniel took the kids from the home of a family friend. He then sent word to Cora that if she wanted to see them ever again she would have to divorce Mark and come back to him. The council divorced her from Mark and remarried her to Daniel in an instant.

To keep a better eye on her, Daniel moved her into a tiny trailer next to Sara's house. She had no running water, so she pulled a garden hose across the street and into the trailer. "Sara would come in and say everything was hers and that she could come in any time she wanted," Cora remembers. "Then she would take the hose away."

As winter set in, the family began freezing in the unheated trailer. Cora's 15- year-old son decided he'd seen his mother and siblings suffer enough and left for St. George to get a job. When he had enough money to get an apartment, he sent for them to join him. "I remember just laying on the carpet in that apartment and crying," she says. "It had no furniture but it was warm."

After one of her daughters attempted suicide, Cora learned that Daniel had raped the daughter. "That was the end of it for me," she says. "[I went on] a fact-finding mission, and I learned Daniel had been a rapist for more than 30 years."

In St. George, Cora continued to seek a spiritual community and went to the local Mormon bishop. "I tried to be part of the LDS church," she says. "After all, I'd had all my kids baptized LDS even though we belonged to a split-off from it." But Cora's affiliation with the mainstream church soured when she asked the bishop about polygamy. "He said, 'We'll all have to live polygamy someday,' and then I thought, 'I'm going to have to go through Hell again?' That finished it for me," says Cora. "The Mormon leaders get upset when people live polygamy now; but then they say, 'We'll live it later. It will be different then.' It can never be different. It's a farce."

Now in her 50s, Cora lives in Las Vegas with a daughter. Her two youngest children live with their father and another sister near Colorado City. Cora continues to derive pleasure from her art work and hopes her fairyland story will be made into a movie for children.

Cora Fischer is the only name that has not been changed in this story.

10.

Fear of things invisible is the
natural seed of that which every one
in himself calleth religion.
—Thomas Hobbes, "Leviathan," 1651

BRENDA

Faces of absent children peer from picture frames hanging on the living room walls in Brenda Bowman's Salt Lake City home. Brenda has not seen her two sons and daughter in more than four years.

Brenda lost her children to her polygamous ex-husband, who moved them to Big Horn County, Wyoming, and split them between his other wives. Once in a while, she talks to them on the phone when her ex-sister-wives don't hang up before the children get on the line. They cry when they talk to her. They tell her about abuses, both physical and sexual. Sometimes the wives take the phone and tell Brenda that her children are 500 miles away and there's nothing she can do about it. They tell her that her children's lives are going on without her. Then they hang up.

Brenda was born into the Mormon fundamentalist polygamist group popularly known as "the Allreds" or the Apostolic United Brethren (AUB). Her father was originally a member of the LeBaron group but converted to the Allred group and married Brenda's mother, who became the second of his two wives.

Brenda's most vivid memories of her childhood are the horrible beatings her father inflicted on his 20 children. "My brothers would get head slams from my father," she remembers. "Heads slammed into one another, into the table, onto the ground. I still have a scar on my backside from a beating."

At the age of 18 and stubbornly avoiding marriage, Brenda ran away. Church members found her and tried to change her mind and bring her back. "I didn't have any friends out in the world," she explains. "And they'd come and tell me how much they wanted me back, how it was for my own good and that I'd go to hell if I didn't. So I did what I thought I was supposed to do." To ensure that Brenda's position back in the church would be cemented, a quick relationship followed by marriage was arranged for her with 30-year-old Martin, a man who already had two wives.

Martin moved his wives into trailers far outside of Lovell, Wyoming, where ten other families of the group were dispersed. "The only time we saw the others was on Sunday for church in one of the trailers," says Brenda. "We were all really isolated and I was scared." Within this isolation, the wives did as they were told, holding their husband up as a prophet in his own right. Martin insisted that he had received a revelation from God telling him that he was the Davidic King who would come in the last days, as spoken of in the book of Isaiah. "Everything he said was the spoken word of a prophet," remembers Brenda. "And we believed it was true."

Brenda's sister-wives were in their late 20s and early 30s and not at all happy about their husband's teenage bride. What's more, Brenda's husband wasn't in love with her, marrying her out of duty to the religion. "He would tell me that he couldn't love me and that I was crazy," she says. "And then we would have family 'debriefing sessions' where the three of them would take turns ripping me apart." Brenda says that her personality went underground at that time. "I began to believe that

I was worth nothing," she says. "I lost the sense of humor that I'd always had as a teenager."

While there was no love between Brenda and her husband, he was still duty bound by the religion to have children by her. "He told me he would decide when there would be anything physical between us," she says. "The religion says sex is supposed to be the woman's decision, but it's not. Not even close."

During her pregnancies, Brenda received no prenatal care because the religion does not believe in doctors. "I got to see the Allred midwife in Salt Lake twice [for her first pregnancy]," she says. "She'd check my heart and blood pressure."

Brenda had grown tired of living with women who hated the sight of her and whose children rummaged though her personal things. She wanted her own space, and found a housekeeping job at a hospital in Lovell. By the time the baby was born, she was living in her own trailer. "I paid for it with my own money and rebuilt the kitchen, which had been torn out."

Nine months after the birth of her baby, Martin decided the family had to move to a more remote part of Wyoming. "He sold my trailer and let me keep $1,000," says Brenda. "I was pregnant again; but I got a new job and used the $1,000 for a down payment on a little house, and I made my monthly payments."

Brenda's pregnancy ended in miscarriage, and she hemorrhaged for more than four hours without any medical attention. "Martin called the midwife in Salt Lake and then took me to one of my sister-wives to watch over me," she says. "He went to bed, and the next day he left for two weeks."

Like Brenda, the other wives were faring for themselves and their children. Just the same, Martin wanted to make sure he wasn't obligated to contribute and called a family debriefing session. "He told us that he was sick of us and would do nothing for us," she says. "He said we had to take care of ourselves, and he'd just come and go as he liked." Though the women were supposedly on their own, as priesthood holder, Martin dictated their daily decisions and at one point decided another move was in order. "He sold my house and kept all the money," says Brenda. "From there, we moved to Utah's West Desert, where a lot of other members are living." The Allred colony is 200 miles out into the desert with the last 50 miles being dirt road.

During the time she was living in a desert shack with only a bedroom, kitchen and bathroom, Brenda became pregnant again. To make money, she took in children as a baby-sitter. "We had no choices over what he did or what we did," she explains. "We just had to keep our mouths shut and be happy." What Martin did next was to marry two more wives.

In the midst of this, one of Brenda's sister-wives gave birth to a stillborn child who was buried in the group's makeshift cemetery. "Some time ago, Owen [Allred] asked the county for a permit to put in a cemetery but they turned him down," explains Brenda. "So he just put one in anyway."

Baby-sitting wasn't bringing in enough money, so Brenda switched to working for a home health agency, eventually earning her certification. "Martin would take my checks and deposit them in his account," she says. "I'm working, he's taking the money and my kids are starving and malnourished. Then I got pregnant again."

The night Brenda delivered her third child was a nightmare that continues to generate painful memories. After three days of on and off labor, she went to spend the night with her sister, who also lived in the West Desert. "I got up in the night to go to the bathroom," remembers

Brenda. "My water broke, and the cord and a foot came out with it." Brenda screamed for her sister to call for help; but, before paramedics arrived, the midwife came and wouldn't let them come in. After the baby was safely delivered, the midwife wouldn't let the paramedics take Brenda and the newborn to the hospital. "She kept telling them that this is the way we do things," she says. "They asked me what I wanted to do, and I went along with the midwife because I didn't want to get stuck with a bill. Martin sure wouldn't pay for it."

However Brenda paid a price for her decision. The baby became deathly ill with an infection. After five weeks Brenda got him to a doctor in Salt Lake who told her the baby was near death with his vital signs at a critical stage. After a brief stay in the hospital, she brought him home and nurtured him to good health.

A good opportunity for returning to civilization came when Brenda's father became ill and was in need of round the clock care as he lay dying at his home near Salt Lake. "He had cancer and had broken his back, and I could be of some help if I lived there." While caring for her father, she found that she could continue working at her job visiting patients if she could find day care for her children. "Martin insisted that only members of our religion watch the children," she says. "Child care took half my paycheck, while Martin made $11 an hour and didn't pay a cent." It was at this point in Brenda's struggles that something changed. "You know how it is when something hits you and you just know? That's how it was," she says. "I was so tired of it that I decided that I wasn't going back. I told him I had changed, and he told me that I was on a one-way track to hell."

The same church members who had found her when she ran away as a teen started to work on her once more. "I had fallen in love with Lewis, the man who was my father's hospice nurse, and they told me I'd be better off with a drunk," she remembers. "These people are so good at manipulation." But Brenda held her ground and, after her father's death, she told Martin she was moving to Salt Lake permanently. "I said I was done, and it didn't even hurt for me to walk away," she says. "The only reason I stayed at all was because I was afraid of going to hell. I'm still working on that brainwashing about hell."

At the time Brenda was ridding herself of Martin, she was still very much invested in the religion. Though her marriage as third wife was not legal, she continued to believe that it was binding from a religious standpoint. "I went to Owen and asked for a release from the marriage, but he wouldn't give it to me," she says. "Then Martin lied to him and told him that I was sleeping with another man, so Owen released Martin from the marriage."

Brenda continued to see Lewis, who was doing all he could to respect her feelings toward her religion. Oddly, Allred began to take interest in their relationship. "Owen kept insisting that we should get married as soon as possible," she says. "He had his reasons that we'd find out about later."

After Brenda and Lewis were married, Martin began a siege of harassment against the two. "He'd sit in his car in front of our house, call me at work and call the house and demand the kids," she says. "I filed a protective order and it was as useless as toilet paper, and then I was scared that I'd go to hell for filing the protective order." But when she filed a paternity suit to obtain support and permanent custody of the children, she and Lewis truly did find hell.

The couple hired an attorney but soon found they could not afford him. Then they discovered that their marriage disqualified them from legal aid. "Owen knew that if I was married, I would have a harder time qualifying for legal aid," she surmises. "That's why he pushed the marriage."

The children came home from one visitation with their father with the youngest having bruises from the top of his back to his lower legs. The next thing she and Lewis knew, Martin had called the DCFS with an allegation of child abuse against them. "DCFS substantiated the charges because Lewis admitted that he sometimes spanks the kids," says Brenda. "But there were no bruises when the kids left to go see their dad."

Case workers doing a family preservation evaluation monitored Brenda, Lewis and the children for six months and reported that their situation was fine. However, the relationship between Brenda and the custody evaluators became strained, especially after they tried to pressure Brenda into utilizing a privately owned and operated company called Will Wind. The state contracts with several such facilities for child visitation transfers between estranged parents. Will Wind, like many businesses in the state, is owned and operated by polygamists. "I just wouldn't deal with them anymore," she says. "So they said I had a temper."

In court, Brenda and Lewis were without an attorney for the first of three appearances. By contrast, Martin had two attorneys who are commonly hired by the Allred group. Brenda feels that she was outgunned by more than just highly paid attorneys. "DCFS and the guardian ad litem [attorney appointed for the children] used polygamy as a weapon to fight us," she says. "It was his big defense and everyone was all for polygamy." Brenda argued that if Martin took the kids, they would live in filthy conditions without water or electricity. His attorneys countered that he couldn't help his poverty because he is a polygamist and should not be punished for it. "They said that polygamy has been practiced around the world and only now are people in this country trying to make it unacceptable," she says. "Then the guardian ad litem testified that living in polygamy would not be harmful to the children." Brenda believes that the guardian ad litem was biased toward polygamy. "She was hell bent and even confronted me with it," says Brenda. "She said, 'You believe you had strength to get out. Well, your kids are staying in.'" Brenda says that the judge, whom she believed to be Mormon, simply brushed her off when she told the court about Martin's belief that he's the Davidic King from the Book of Isaiah.

On the third day of court, Brenda had scraped enough money together to employ a new attorney. "He treated the whole thing like it was a game, telling me that he thought my case was fun," she says. "Losing my children is serious. There was nothing fun about that." In the end, Martin got full custody and was court ordered to bring the children to spend every weekend with her. "At first he'd write from the West Desert that they couldn't come because his truck was broke down or some other reason," she says. "I'd get them only every now and then."

Reeling from the vast changes in her life and the devastating loss of her children, Brenda had time to reflect about the community she'd left behind. She took off her religious undergarments. It was a decision, she says, that was very difficult for her. Feelings boiled over one morning when she picked up the Salt Lake morning newspaper to read a letter to the editor from Owen Allred. His letter described how his flock had no problems of sexual abuse. He wanted to inform the Utah public that he took measures within his own people to properly handle anything that was unseemly. "I could not believe the lies, so I wrote a letter to the paper describing how I had been in the religion, had seen sexual abuse everywhere and how it's covered up when they find out about it," she says. "It got published, and within the month, the court nailed me with having to have supervised visitation with my kids, even though Lewis and I have two of our own who are doing well."

The new visitation arrangement didn't last any longer than her supposed weekend visitations. With the children now living in Wyoming, seeing them seems an impossible dream. The calls between mother and children are few, and Brenda worries that they're being treated the way she was once treated in the family. "On the few visits I had in the beginning, I'd hear my kids say that they're not worth anything," she says. "Now they're back there with nothing—no books, no music and they don't even have me."

11

*Evils which are patiently endured
when they seem inevitable become intolerable
once the idea of escape from them is suggested.*
—Alexis de Tocqueville

CONNIE

As an infant, Connie Rugg was never held. She was never rocked or hugged. She heard no lullabies, no loving response to her baby coos. She grew from infancy into childhood looking out at the world from the inside of a crib. When Connie cried, her mother slapped her until she stopped.

As the sixth wife of Ortell Kingston, her mother had learned to deny her feelings in order to survive her husband sleeping with other women. With no feelings left for any of her 13 children, her mother left Connie and her siblings bereft of a mother's love. "She would say that she didn't want her children to become too attached or to be spoiled. I grew up depressed and angry with my mother," Connie says. "I wanted affection, but my mother wouldn't give it to me."

Looking back at her childhood, the petite redhead remembers being suicidal beginning in kindergarten. "I'd see 'outsider' children and wonder why they would run and play," she says. "I'd think, 'Why run for fun?'" She eventually went as far as the 10th grade, but chronic depression caused her to miss too many days to keep up with her classmates. She finally left high school all together.

The men in the Kingston group do little or nothing to support their many wives and children. Often women turn to welfare as "single" mothers. Others work for meager wages in Kingston-owned businesses. All are expected to live in destitute conditions in order to "refine their souls" into a more Christ-like existence. They are told that if they sacrifice now, when Christ returns, the wicked will be destroyed, and they will be given their pick of the beautiful homes left behind.

Connie's mother was told by church leaders that she could spend only $10 per person per month. "We lived on beans, rice and oatmeal; and late at night, my mom and others in the group would raid the dumpsters behind the grocery stores," says Connie. "Some of the men go every night to the dumpsters. They take produce, rotting and all, and demand that the wives not let anything go to waste. That's the most support those women get."

Home for Connie and her 12 siblings was a run-down two bedroom house at a coal yard owned by the Kingston group in Murray, Utah, a suburb of Salt Lake City. Shelves were removed from the kitchen pantry to make room for two sets of bunk beds. At one time, another of her father's wives lived with them until she had her fourth child.

Like all Kingston children who are not born from first wives, Connie had no idea who her father was. She and her siblings were told that their father was a truck driver named Steven Joseph Johnson, who would come home to them someday. "At the coal yard, truck drivers would drive in and out all the time; and we always wondered if our father would be among them. So we kids were friendly to them and would get them to honk their air horns by pulling our arm up and down," remembers Connie. "One day, a truck driver blew his horn and waved at me before I had the chance to pull my arm; so I thought he was our father and that was his way of showing it." Connie ran home as fast as she could to meet her father who had at long last returned to his family. She reached the house in bitter disappointment, finding no one waiting for her.

The tenets of the LDS-based religion were a constant in Connie's life as she dutifully read the *Book of Mormon*, the Bible and the teachings of the Kingston leaders. She memorized the daily "Memory Gems" and also attended church, where their prophet spoke every Sunday. But Connie had an insatiable curiosity that was creating waves of doubt in her mind. "I read those scriptures and then went further and read Mormon history and the history of Christianity," she says. "I realized these ideas were opposite of what I thought humanity should be. Joseph Smith was just like the Kingstons." An undermined faith was just one more crack in the shaky ground Connie was standing on. Children in the group are part of the Kingston workforce from an early age, and Connie was not spared from hard child labor. Since the start of her sixth grade year, she had been working for the Kingston businesses, paying all of her own expenses on the 25 cents an hour that went into her account. "My mother had so many children and there was so much dire need," she says. "I bought my own clothes and shoes and tried to stay away because I couldn't face the dirtiness and hunger of the younger children."

The distraction of work helped her escape the loveless home life during the days, and in the evenings, she would stay away by tagging along with her brother and his friend. "I built a romantic relationship with my brother's friend because he was the first person who I felt really liked me," she says. "I didn't love him; but it felt good when Robert would hug me, and I knew he'd do anything for me."

Connie's mother noticed the blossoming romance but, like all mothers in the Kingston group, she wanted her daughter to marry into the royal Kingston bloodline, which the group believes traces back to Jesus Christ. Although Robert belonged to the group, he was not a Kingston.

"I was 17, and my mother said that no teenage girl had the right to choose a husband," says Connie. "I remember thinking, 'Oh yeah, we'll see about that.'" While Connie was setting her mind against having an arranged marriage, her mother was planning the wedding. "She said, 'You don't need to know who you're going to marry. Just pick a date and show up, and you'll find out on the wedding day who it is.'"

In an effort to prevent Connie and Robert's romance from thwarting the upcoming wedding plans, her mother forbade them from seeing each other. "I had a key to the bathroom and I'd go in there at midnight, lock the door and turn on the shower," says Connie. "Everyone thought I was taking long late-night showers, but I'd be gone out the window to meet Robert."

One night the pair stayed out too long. When they realized that Connie's shower ruse was over, they drove to Elko, Nevada, to get married. Connie was barely 17, and getting married, even in Nevada, was impossible. At a dead end and with an old car that wouldn't drive another inch, the two stayed in Elko for three days before they called Connie's mother to let her know where they were.

As Connie watched her mother's arrival from the hotel window, she saw that her cousin, Roger, had also come. "Roger always wanted to marry me from the time he was 30 and I was 14," she says. "He told me that he'd received direction to marry me, and he was acceptable to my mom because he was a Kingston."

Robert stayed behind in Elko with the broken-down car, while Connie was escorted back to Salt Lake by her mother and amorous cousin. "My mother slept while Roger explained how after we got married, his first wife would stay home with the kids and be a servant while he and I traveled," she says. "I found him disgusting in that he could talk that way about Jaynie. I couldn't accept him, that life or any of them."

Connie listened to Roger all through the long ride back to her mother's home, realizing what a horrible life her mother had lived. "I thought, 'How could any mother wish that same life on her daughter?'" She says, "I thought about my choices. I could either go along with them, leave with Robert again or I could commit suicide." Having already ruled out going along with the rules of the religion, she decided leaving with Robert would cause too much pain and trouble. "I had no idea that anyone would really care if I was dead," she says. "My death would end the pain for me and my mother, family and friends. It was my only choice."

Back at her mother's house, Roger continued to court Connie, who recoiled at his idea of their future life together. "On his wife's birthday, he took her and me out to dinner; then he dropped her off and took me for a ride," she says. "Here he was telling me again how we would have this exciting life with her as the servant. On her birthday."

Connie could tolerate the unwanted attentions from Roger only because she was planning to be rid of him soon. With a giant bottle of aspirin hidden away, she was waiting for a night when she knew her mother would be sleeping late the next morning. "I got a glass of water and took handfuls of aspirin at a time with tiny amounts of water," she remembers. "Then I laid down to sleep."

But lying in bed and thinking, she began getting scared and called Robert to tell him what she'd done. "He came over with his mother and drove me to the ER," she says. "They pumped my stomach. The aspirin came out looking like marshmallows. The doctor asked me why I did it and I told him, 'Because I had a headache.'"

Connie stayed in the hospital through the night, but her mother insisted that she come home and go back to work the next day. "She was angry. No other emotion but anger," says Connie. "I went to work, but I was so weak I couldn't walk."

There was one person in Connie's life who felt emotion about her suicide attempt. "Robert was devastated and hurt. He cried," she says. "It felt good to have someone care so much, so I decided not to give in to the suicidal feelings. That was really hard because the suicidal urges were stronger than ever because of how my mother was treating me."

Continuing to work, Connie was now involved in the bookkeeping for the multi-million dollar Kingston business empire. "They have their own banking system and their own private books," she says. "We made up a false set of books for the IRS."

Connie and Robert made one more attempt to run away together, driving to Idaho Falls where Robert's sister lived after her own flight from the Kingston church years before. But soon after they arrived, Connie's brother was killed in an accident. When the news reached them, they returned to Utah to mourn. "I decided then that instead of running away, I'd wait until I turned 18 and then I'd leave."

Just one day after her 18th birthday, Connie packed her belongings and Robert loaded them into his car. Her mother and Roger sat and watched. The two drove to Idaho Falls and were married at the courthouse.

After growing up in the Kingston group, the couple had more to cope with than just the marriage. "I was living in a state of shock, believing I was going to hell," she says. "But I was happy and thrilled to be away. Every day was an adventure."

To help her navigate in this new world and put her past in perspective, Connie decided to begin therapy. "My feelings had been so suppressed; and as new feelings developed, I was aware of each one," she says. "They felt like fingers grabbing on to me. I was amazed at the new experience of having emotion."

As Connie's life expanded and her self-awareness exploded, she and Robert began growing apart. He continued to insist on the male privilege and supremacy that he'd enjoyed growing up in the religion's priesthood. In addition, Connie had given birth to two children in two years while working part-time. "Robert wouldn't do a thing, not for himself or at home; and he wanted me to do everything for him," she says. "He was too much to take care of, so I decided life would be easier without him."

With the marriage over, Connie became a single, working mother. After several years of carrying the heavy load of single parenthood with little resources for childcare, her mother enticed her back to Utah with the offer of helping look after the children. "I knew the group would never bother with my son as far as getting him into the religion," she says. "And my daughter is too strong willed to buy into it."

But things were different for her younger siblings. Connie watched helplessly as her little sister, Andrea, was married to their half-brother, Jason. He was 16 and she was 14. "She got pregnant and became very swollen and sick," says Connie. "My mother knew it was toxemia, but Jason and his mom said they were taking care of it."

Kingston members are paranoid of the medical profession and rarely seek medical attention except in an extreme emergency. Women in the group do not receive prenatal care, and husbands or women's fathers deliver babies. The paranoia stems from a belief that doctors don't want women to have more than four children and perform unwanted hysterectomies or administer birth control.

Andrea became so critically ill from toxemia that Jason summoned her mother. "By the time Mom arrived, Andrea was blind because swelling in her brain had crushed her optic nerve. She was delirious and screaming for help," says Connie. "Our mother took her to the hospital where they had to cut the top of her skull off to relieve the swelling. There were two blood clots the size of lemons in her brain."

The baby boy, delivered by emergency Caesarean section, weighed only one pound, eleven ounces. Andrea died in the hospital 14 days later of eclampsia, a condition that could have been prevented with prenatal care. On her death certificate, Ortell Kingston was not revealed as her father. The fictional truck driver Steven Joseph Johnson was recorded instead. It was five years before Connie and her family were to learn that the child Andrea delivered has cerebral palsy. "It's not uncommon that no one would discuss it," says Connie. "They're so closed, even among themselves."

Connie visits Andrea's grave and is grateful for the choices she has today. It has been 23 years since Connie chose to leave the life she was born into. "Someone who's mentally healthy wouldn't live this lifestyle," she says. "You have to be sick to fall into this to begin with. These people came together because of their mental illnesses."

12.

*Those who do not remember the past are
condemned to repeat it.*
—George Santyana

CINDY

It is boggling to Cindy Hammer when she reflects on the unexpected turn her life has taken the last few years. After finishing a college education with honors, she was on her way to a bright career that would provide a better life for herself and her two sons. But those plans were seriously derailed.

Cindy was raised as a Pentecostal Christian in Oklahoma. By 28, she was a single mother of two and in college. It was there that she and her friends joined the Mormon Church after taking missionary lessons. Having struggled through a long period of involvement with only work, school and motherhood, she jumped at a chance to take a break. "In the summer of 1996, before I was to finish my last six weeks of college, I went on a road trip with a girlfriend while my boys visited their father," she says. "We drove to Utah and stopped one night at the Yogi Bear Campground in Manti."

The campground was owned by a group of Mormon fundamentalist polygamists known as the True and Living Church of Jesus Christ of Saints of the Last Days (TLC). In 1990, the church's prophet, Jim Harmston, had settled in the tiny historical Mormon town of Manti while a "gathering" of followers flocked around him. In the spirit of the early Mormon United Order belief, followers willingly gave all their financial assets to help build the new religion, which included buying the old, run-down campground.

"The guys running the campground wanted to talk to us, and so we ended up staying a week and a half," she says. "They talked about 'the gathering' and Mormon history. They also showed us hieroglyphics on a mountain behind the Mormon Temple. The Mormons in the area and the TLC all think it's Lamanite writing."

The women were introduced to the group, which has a membership of approximately 300 men, women and children. All homes where TLC members live bear a sign above the door that reads, "Holiness To The Lord." Homes purchased by the TLC have a sign posted in the front yard reading, "Consecrated Property of The True and Living Church of Jesus Christ of Saints of the Last Days."

When the two women decided it was time to leave, they were pressed by members to remain in Manti. "After working so hard for my education, I couldn't not go back with just six weeks left," she says. "So we left, but they wrote letters to us; and then a couple of women came out to stay with me to try to get me and my friend to go back and join."

Members of the TLC were also sending her reading materials, which included *The Teachings of The Prophet Joseph Smith* and two days' worth of Harmston's Models, an intensive TLC course. "I didn't have a job to walk into after college, so I told them, 'If you want me, then figure out a way to get me there,'" she says. "So the TLC sent me three plane tickets. In September, my sons and I flew to Utah."

Back in Manti, Cindy attended the intensive Models conversion process day after day, without food or breaks and with very little sleep. Her boys were enrolled in the church's school. She was saturated with rhetoric of the TLC religion, forcing back her doubts about leaving her family in Oklahoma. "I was torn but felt good about how welcoming they were and about the blessing they gave me, telling me I made the right decision," she says. "There was so much energy. It was a spiritual feast, and I felt like the Savior was there."

Cindy was baptized and then promptly courted by Chuck, who had only one wife. "We had sex all the time before the marriage, but Chuck said it wasn't breaking his covenants because he hadn't 'spilled his seed' during our encounters," she remembers. "When I married him, I became his second wife; two weeks later, he invited another woman to be his third wife."

Soon after Chuck took his third wife, Cindy got a call from her brother in Oklahoma telling her that their mother was dying. Within three days, she was dead. Cindy also discovered she was pregnant. While Cindy was away for her mother's funeral, Chuck moved into the third wife's bedroom. "When I got back, they called a family meeting to tell us she would be in charge of us like a mother over us," says Cindy. "The next morning, they went to 'Prayer in Robes,' and I went to talk to the church leaders about my problem with the third wife."

The leaders told Cindy they would pray about the problem. After their prayers, they told her that her husband and his third wife had been husband and wife in another life. They said that, in one of his "multiple probations" (see glossary) he had been former Mormon Church president Heber J. Grant and the third wife had been one of Grant's wives, Lucy Stringham. Cindy was directed to take her rightful, subordinate place.

Being too independent to have another wife in charge of her life, Cindy told Chuck that she wanted out through the church's "Rescue Me" program. The program allows a woman to leave an unhappy union provided she is soon remarried. Often, a wife or husband will have a revelation telling them that they should be married to someone else. In such a case, they rely on the Rescue Me program to help them make the switch. "The men in the TLC change wives like people change underwear," says Cindy. "The children belong to the mother and the father is absolved of having anything to do with them."

Her marriage was dissolved by church leaders, and she was offered up as new wife material. "As a woman, you have to be married to someone," she says. "You can't be a single woman because a husband introduces his wives to Christ."

She was soon married to her second husband, Bruce, as his fourth wife, and moved with her sons into a seven-bedroom, two-bathroom residence that was home to five adults and 30 children. The first wife contrived numerous behavioral and dietary rules for the household. "After a month and a half, all hell broke loose over me giving my son a peanut butter sandwich," she remembers. "I was breaking rules, and it wouldn't be the last time."

But the adults didn't have time to sort out family problems. With the older children looking after the younger ones, they threw themselves into numerous religious ceremonies. "We were always doing baptisms for the dead. We baptized historical Mormon figures and world figures all the way back to Adam," she says. "Some were talking to those on the other side of the veil, and those conversations were taped and had to be transcribed."

At age 15, Angie, a pretty blonde girl, was being groomed to marry the 58-year-old prophet (Jim Harmston) and give birth to the "One Mighty and Strong" mentioned in the Mormon *Doctrine and Covenants*. "I was helping Angie transcribe the tapes and I had to go to her bedroom for transcribing, so I knew all about her secret marriage to Jim," says Cindy. "Angie was sleeping with and taking lessons on sexual techniques from one of Jim's wives (who, along with other female members of the group, were former members of the Shreeve groups and on the Utah sex offender list), while being groomed to marry Jim herself."

With little to no supervision, the children began inventing ways to entertain one another. They were caught in the act of exposing themselves one evening just as the adults came home. "Our church parenting classes taught that if you spare the rod you spoil the child; so of course they had to be whipped," she says. "I stood in horror as the children received twenty whacks with two-inch thick dowel rods."

Cindy was told by her husband to "get over it" when she expressed her feelings about the beatings. But, by January of 1998, the arguments between Cindy and the other adults were increasing. "Bruce said he'd no longer sleep with me because of my problems with anger," she says. "Then the kids were caught exposing themselves to each other again and got another beating. When I objected, he told me and my kids to get out."

In October, Cindy gave birth to a daughter, and the man who had just thrown her out offered to give the new baby his last name. "Bruce said that he couldn't have us in his house, but signed the birth certificate and left," she says. "Two weeks later he hired an attorney to have his name removed from the birth certificate, and his attorney ordered a paternity test. As though no one knew she was from Chuck." Cindy never was told the results of the paternity test or whether Bruce's name was removed from her daughter's birth certificate.

Several men offered to marry Cindy after her second marriage was dissolved, but she held off the advances, knowing she would eventually have to remarry. "Then Jim got a revelation about preparing people for the Lord. All single women with 'white aprons'—otherwise known as members of the Church of the First Born—had to be married right away in a new order," she says. "I had the white apron."

The new order meant that Cindy's new husband would have stewardship over her to teach her to be a better mother and wife. She was again married, this time as a second wife. "I was crying and freaking out on my wedding day," she remembers. "But, as usual, I thought that God says it will help me in my progression."

As part of the push to ready the members for the coming of the Lord, Harmston took eight more wives himself for a total of 17 wives. Advanced endowment sessions [see glossary] were stepped up, and a revelation proclaiming the date of the Lord's return was declared. "Jesus was to come to Manti on March 25, 2000," says Cindy. "We were all busy preparing for the 'Feast of the Bridegroom.'"

The members obtained numerous credit cards and maxed them out buying china, silverware, goblets, food, a large freezer, chocolate desserts and fresh flowers. Jesus was to come to the TLC members, and together they would cleanse the Mormon temple in Manti and feast together on the third floor. "When Jesus didn't come after we waited all night in the Assembly Hall, Jim told us to go home and find out why and to ask, 'Is it me that kept him from coming?'" she says. "Early the next day, we reassembled and stayed until four the next morning hashing out our individual sins and asking forgiveness."

According to Harmston, the arrival of Jesus will now be at a later date. In the meantime, TLC members continue to prepare themselves. "Jim has announced that some of his wives are resurrected ["translated"; see glossary] beings, and one is an eternal mother on planet Altera where the three Nephites [from the *Book of Mormon*] are," says Cindy. At one point, Cindy was told that she and her children belonged to Jeremiah, one of the three Nephites.

TLC followers believe that Harmston and one of his wives are parents to children on other orbs and planets and, when the earth is cleansed, these planetary bodies will join with the earth. This wife is said to be in contact with the families on the other planets and speaks with them, dispersing messages. Further, Harmston teaches that when he goes to sleep he visits other planets or lives other probations and that all the members could have these same experiences if they didn't have doubts. "In his revelations, he tells that there are celestial rooms where our main bodies lay down and sleep so we can live other probations," says Cindy. "We can go live on earth or other planets, then discard our bodies as though they are clothes and wake up in our celestial room with our main bodies."

In the meantime, Cindy says, "Don Peterson, one of Harmston's 12 apostles has been assigned to rewrite the esoteric history of the world because history has been tainted. Only revelation will give the true history about other probations of who and where members have been."

While living under the stewardship of her new husband, Cindy and her three children were struggling to survive on welfare and a minimum wage job. "No husband in the TLC ever supports a wife and her kids," she says. "The men are busy building up the kingdom. The few who do have jobs get paid under the table with just a minimal amount showing on a paycheck for the benefit of the IRS. The women take minimum wage jobs in the area and almost everyone is on welfare."

Eventually, the doctrines of the religion were getting harder and harder for her to reconcile. Questions and inconsistences became increasingly difficult to ignore. One day while she was getting ready for work, the television was turned to a historical program chronicling the more than 900 followers of Jim Jones who moved with him to Guyana and, at his direction, committed mass suicide. "I thought, 'Oh my gosh, that's going on here,'" she says.

From that day forward, Cindy began quietly planning her escape with her children, hiding a few belongings at work each day and researching leads on job opportunities. With funds given to her by Tapestry, she was finally able to make her break.

In the middle of a warm summer night, she filled her car with the few possessions she had hidden away, tucked the children into blankets and drove out of town. By daybreak she had crossed the Utah state line. She never looked back.

13.

Less power to religion,
the greater power to knowledge.
—Hypatia Bradlaugh Bonner, *Testament*, 1942

SYLVIA

It is a long way from Hamburg, Germany, to the tiny polygamist community of Pinesdale, Montana. But the massive journey Sylvia Jessop would make proved to be much more than geographical.

Sylvia's father joined the Mormon Church while still a teenager in Germany, where he also met her mother, a long-time church member. The young couple was married in the LDS Swiss Temple and began their family with dreams of emigrating to the United States.

By 1963, Sylvia's father was working in New York City and had saved enough money to send for his wife and two daughters. Sylvia remembers little of her Atlantic crossing at age three except that she spoke only German and she nearly fell overboard after climbing on the rail.

New York was only a stop on the way to their ultimate destination. They were intent on coming west to the hub of Mormondom; and by the time Sylvia was eight years old, the family was living in Salt Lake City.

At his work, Sylvia's father spent hours talking with a co-worker who was a member of the Allred group. One council member in the church, a man with ten wives, recited scriptures and early Mormon Church history in ways that Sylvia's father found rapturous. Her father heard how the early church attempted and failed to live the United Order and how the Apostolic United Brethren (AUB) were working toward living it successfully. He knew the early Mormon Church embraced, fought for and eventually gave up polygamy, and now he heard John Ray speaking about the celestial principle as never having left God's chosen people.

"In 1969, when I was ten years old, I was baptized into the AUB," says Sylvia. "And by age 12, our family and other church members went to settle in Montana."

Nestled in the Bitter Root Valley, Pinesdale sits just northwest of Hamilton, surrounded on every side by national forests. The town is approximately one-and-a-half miles long and three-fourths of a mile wide and is home to roughly 1,000 residents of the AUB. In addition to large homes and numerous trailers, there is a post office, fire department, city hall, country store, school and Sylvia's father's cabinet shop. "In the beginning, everyone felt a 'revival' kind of excited enthusiasm," remembers Sylvia. "A lot of people lived in tents at first. We all felt we were on a God-sent mission to build up the perfect community." In the late 1960s and early 1970s, a large number of disaffected Mormons joined the AUB and moved to Pinesdale. "These were primarily monogamous couples who came to the community for more wives," says Sylvia.

Building a polygamist community requires quick marriages and prolific procreation, and the members of Pinesdale were anxious to do their duty. "Girls who were 14, 15 and 16 became the second wives of many men. If a man married a council member's daughter, he then had the right political connections in town," says Sylvia. "One guy asked to court me and I told a girlfriend about it. She got furious and said she was secretly married to him. She was only 14. A lot of men took young girls in the night to get secretly married."

The high school, now known as Pinesdale Academy, started out in different homes with several women in the group serving as teachers.

Only the children of "old timers" or council members were allowed to attend public school. Sylvia was not one of them. "I had no high school education but was home-schooled, going from basement to basement," says Sylvia. "I remember the 30 plus-year-old principal taking my 16-year-old girlfriend out into the hall at school one day and asking her to marry him."

In the AUB, as in all Mormon fundamentalist polygamist groups, religion dominates the lives of members. "The rhetoric was constant with many long meetings that included firesides, Sunday worship, women's meetings, teen meetings and children's meetings, consisting of Boy Scouts, family and personal scripture reading and religion classes in school," says Sylvia. "Everyone had pictures of those in the line of priesthood authority in their homes, starting with Joseph Smith and going to Owen Allred."

When Sylvia was nearing her 13th birthday, her father married Vera, a 14-year-old girl, as his second wife. "Rulon Allred, the now-martyred prophet, married that child to my father," says Sylvia. "I can remember my mother sewing her wedding dress. It was green dotted Swiss."

With a new wife crammed into the family trailer, privacy was at a minimum. "My mom would walk past the two of them french kissing on the couch. One night I found my mother hitting herself with a hair brush so she wouldn't think about it," says Sylvia. "The rest of the time, Mom had to teach Vera home skills like another child. Then Vera had a son right away."

Sylvia's family life was dominated by fighting between sister-wives while the larger community dealt with arguments between factions within the group. "There was a divide between the old timers and the converts brought in by John Ray," says Sylvia. "Things started coming out about sexual abuse, generational incest, inbreeding and covert politics."

Tensions manifested in the mistreatment and scapegoating of young boys. One teen boy was taken by several men intent on meting out punishment for his behavior toward a stepfather. The men stripped the boy naked and attempted, unsuccessfully, to castrate him. Then they poured a purple stain known as Gentian Violet all over him and pinned notes into his body. "I knew three boys who were forced to remain in a potato cellar for three days and nights without food or water, and boys beaten with two-by-fours," says Sylvia.

Though numerous older men proposed to Sylvia during her teen years, she was able to refuse their advances with the support of her father. At age 18, she became the bride of her 19-year-old boyfriend. The two began a family and started building a house so they could leave their tiny trailer. "Robbie wanted a second wife and I struggled with that," says Sylvia. "But it never happened because one day he came home from work really sick."

Although the AUB religion shuns doctors and medicine, the couple sought out a physician, who diagnosed Robbie with colon cancer. "The doctor wanted to operate, but so many church members were fasting and praying that Robbie thought he could heal without surgery," says Sylvia. "The priesthood commanded him to rise and walk in a private Sacrament meeting, and they said if he had enough faith he could be healed." But Robbie didn't heal, and by the time he finally consented to the surgery, the cancer had spread through his intestines. He died just one day after their second child, a son, was born. "Robbie was the love of my life, and we'd only been married two years and four months."

As Sylvia was grieving the loss of her husband while trying to care for her newborn, a friend stopped by late one night with a knitted baby blanket. "She said she was told not to talk to me, but she wanted to say good-bye because she was leaving Pinesdale for good," says Sylvia. "She gave me the blanket and was gone in an instant. I always wondered why she left that way." Years later, Sylvia searched for and made contact with her friend and discovered the story. "Her husband had mutilated her genitals by giving her a clitoridectomy with fishing wire. She took her pictures off the walls and left in the dead of the night."

Within a few months of her husband's death, Sylvia's in-laws approached her with plans for her future. "My father-in-law said I could marry him or any of the remaining 11 sons. Then he jokingly said I would probably think him too old," remembers Sylvia. "My mother-in-law told me that no one would love my kids like one of my husband's brothers; and since Robbie's older brother, Marty, and his wife couldn't have children, I was told he was my best choice and that he was the one I should marry."

Marty then began stopping by Sylvia's trailer to fix things and help her out. "I felt uncomfortable around him, but he asked me to marry him," she says. "I didn't dare say no, so I went to Owen. You don't make decisions without going to Owen. Marty and I went out two times before the wedding and were married just nine months after Robbie's death."

Sylvia had lived in polygamy most of her life and now that she was expected to become a plural wife herself, she was determined to give it her all to make it work.

Her wedding ceremony was a disappointing preview of what was to come. As with the Mormon Church, which believes in sealing marriages for eternity, the AUB maintained that Sylvia was Robbie's wife for eternity and married to Marty for only her remaining time on earth. Hence, she was a "time wife." Any children she would have with Marty would actually belong to Robbie in the afterlife. "I was a 'time wife' so I didn't get wedding pictures or a ring," says Sylvia. "I got a necklace that his first wife, Mara, picked out. I was told that I already had a ring and wedding pictures from before and didn't need them here."

"Mara would constantly tell me that Marty needs to be thinking of Robbie when he's with me," remembers Sylvia. "She tried to control everything at my house."

Having enjoyed an active and passionate sex life with Robbie, Sylvia was disappointed to discover that Marty believed sex should be only for the purpose of having children. Added to this, Mara was working hard to conceive and believed that her chances of pregnancy would be better if Marty did not have sex with Sylvia for two weeks prior to her own fertile time. Sylvia was not told about the theory until several months into the marriage when she angrily confronted Marty for being affectionate only two weeks per month and then cold for two weeks. "During the two weeks of his being cold, I would try harder to be the perfect wife," says Sylvia. "I thought it was my fault he would be cold toward me."

During one evening after the kids were in bed, Sylvia and Marty began kissing. "He put his hands up my blouse and I undid his pants. Then he jumped up saying he had to go to Mara's," says Sylvia. "I cried for hours. I turned him on and he went to finish with her."

In spite of the sexual repression and unorthodox fertility practices, Sylvia continued to find herself pregnant, eventually having five more children. In the meantime, Marty married an additional wife, Sherri. "I had four kids by the time he married his third wife, so I got to move into a house and out of the trailer," says Sylvia. "The other wives would shut me out of their activities. I never was a part of the family no matter how I tried."

During the third month of a seventh pregnancy that Sylvia herself wasn't aware of, she began to miscarry. She was put to bed and given a priesthood blessing as she was hemorrhaging. "Sherri knew I was miscarrying, but she called and told Marty to come home to her house for dinner," remembers Sylvia. "I heard him arguing with her, but then he left. I passed out, so he was called to take me to the hospital." The next day her mother-in-law scolded her for not sharing the news of her pregnancy with her sister-wives.

As a polygamist wife, Sylvia was well-trained in domestic duties. "I sewed all the kids' clothes including the underwear, kept a large garden, baked from scratch and kept a spotless house," she says. "But I was criticized by Mara and Marty for being inconsistent as a parent because I was re-evaluating the use of the corporal punishment that he insisted I use on the kids."

The only time all the wives lived under the same roof was during one cold Montana winter when Marty moved the other wives into Sylvia's house to reduce heating costs. "I'd never leave any sign that Marty and I had spent the night together. I'd clean up and make the bed. I didn't want them to feel bad," Sylvia says. "The two other wives would leave his underwear out on the beds with the blankets all crumpled."

Contentions between Sylvia and Mara had begun early in the marriage with the birth of Sylvia's first child by Marty. "Mara and Marty took my baby from me before I was able to breastfeed her," remembers Sylvia. "Marty would always want to take the baby over to Mara's house; if it wasn't a good time for me or if I needed to feed the baby, I'd be accused of not wanting Mara to see the baby."

When the child was older, Marty decided Sylvia should stop feeding her baby crackers during the long hours of church. "Mara gave the baby a cracker the next Sunday right after I had refused to give her any," says Sylvia. "I told Marty that he should tell Mara not to give April crackers in church, and he said, 'Absolutely not.' So that made me the bad guy to my own child and Mara the good guy."

One day Mara and Marty were having an argument while his mother and Sylvia sat in an adjoining room. "They were arguing about how to discipline my child," says Sylvia. "I started to get up to go in to say something and my mother-in-law grabbed me and wouldn't let me intervene for my own child."

During a subsequent pregnancy, Mara and Sylvia got into a verbal argument. "I wanted to resolve the issue and she wanted to leave, so I sat on her car," says Sylvia. "She sped off down the highway for three miles with me six months pregnant and hanging onto the wipers for dear life."

Through her five pregnancies with Marty, Sylvia was told repeatedly that she was not to name a male child after Marty since she was only a "time wife." Sherri eventually bore eight children, including a boy named Marty. Mara never had any children. "One day Mara asked me to read a letter that her mother wrote to her. It talked about the woman who has children but doesn't deserve them, and then the one who can't but would be the best mother," says Sylvia. "I knew who she meant didn't deserve children, and I knew Mara wanted me to know. I was crushed."

Sylvia lived for her children. The pain she endured taught her to be keenly aware of their feelings and caused her to be vigilant and protective of them. "The kids were drilled that all of them belonged to Robbie, and it hurt my kids born by Marty to think he wasn't their 'real' dad," says Sylvia. "I always told them that they were lucky to have two dads."

Sylvia became more concerned for her children as they witnessed Marty become physically abusive with her. "The kids were afraid. Besides the physical abuse, he was always threatening to leave me and talking about how Joseph Smith had put one of his wives aside," she says. "He'd say he should do the same with me."

In spite of the religious dictum against doctors, Sylvia decided to begin seeing a therapist to deal with her marriage and to reconcile the conflicts she was facing in her day-to-day life. "It's hard to hold the reality of what life really is against what you're told life is." She knew of boys involved in gang rapes but protected under the umbrella of the priesthood. Her own mother-in-law's father married his stepdaughter when she was 16, though he'd raised her as his daughter since she was one year old. She knew one girl who was raped at age 16, then forced to marry another man who was fearful he would never get a wife. "She cried herself to sleep every night for a year," says Sylvia. "And there are all the women living with the thought that their husband is having sex with another woman. I know what it does to them. Many have had mental breakdowns; some wait for their husbands to marry again, with only the satisfaction that the last wife will be the next to break."

Just before the fourth of July, Marty was leaving for a trip to Las Vegas to attend an anti-government meeting on how to not pay taxes. "He would always say something devastating before going on a trip," remembers Sylvia. "This time he said, 'Let's separate.' When he came back, he asked if he was coming to dinner. I said, 'Not that I know of.'" For two weeks, she refused to let him come home, and then agreed to have him come to dinner every three nights.

For one year, Sylvia continued to serve dinner to Marty on the new schedule. At the end of the year, she made four requests. "I asked for a wedding ring, an addition to my house, for him not to tell family members about our fights and not to tell the other wives about our fights," she says. "He told me he'd do none of those things, so I mailed a letter to Owen asking for a release from my marriage."

Allred granted Sylvia a release from her 12-year marriage to Marty in December of 1992. Although she left the church soon after the breakup of her marriage, she has continued to live in the community and in the same house. Her in-laws told her that she had betrayed her covenants to Robbie for leaving Marty. "Most of the time when a woman leaves they don't walk away with their kids, especially if she's a second or third wife," says Sylvia. "I stayed in the community and I think they allowed me to keep the kids because of that, so I was luckier."

Even so, Sylvia had to fight for her kids. "My 13-year-old went to visit my mother-in-law for two weeks and I couldn't get him back. He lived with them until he was 18," she says. "I couldn't call the police because my brother-in-law is the police in Pinesdale. When Marty was being physically abusive, would I have gotten any help?"

Later, Mara took the two older girls to her home without informing Sylvia. "I went over and knocked on the door to bring them back," she says. "I found out she wanted to discuss them living with her. These were my children."

Staying in the house has not been an easy feat either, since the church holds the title to all property and homes in Pinesdale. Sylvia has been fighting a long legal battle against the AUB for the right to stay in the home or be reimbursed for it so she can move to a comparable home outside the community.

She has since returned to school, obtaining her high school equivalency degree, a bachelor's degree in social work and, in 1999, a master's degree. She is now a licensed clinical social worker and continues to live in Pinesdale. Her children have a good relationship with Marty and their grandparents. Some of them have left and married monogamously and some are considering a life in polygamy.

During her years in school, Sylvia volunteered one night a week at a nearby town's domestic violence shelter, where a visual aid known as "The Power of Control Wheel" is used to demonstrate issues of control in domestic violence. "I worked there for four years, and the things I learned helped me see my own life," she says. "The 'Power of Control Wheel' has a part about emotional abuse, and that had a profound effect on me."

As Sylvia continues to grow and change, she hopes to leave Pinesdale one day. In the meantime, she watches the community from a new perspective and is shocked by things she once believed were higher laws. Marty is now an elected judge in Pinesdale, although he has never even attended law school.

"Right now the bishop is in an anti-government militia that believes the government controls the weather. Earlier he was involved with the militia that threatened to bomb the courthouse in Hamilton," she says. "Yet it seems the polygamists have made the larger community think they're such good people. They've infiltrated the schools and other institutions, and the larger community seems to give them more credibility than they give those of us who leave."

Sylvia, Rulon Allred and Owen Allred are the only true names in this story.

14.

Heresy makes for progress.
—Hypatia Bradlaugh Bonner, Reformer, 1897

SHERRIE

Although Sherrie Burnham was not raised with polygamous parents ("my father wasn't 'worthy' enough in name or money for the council to allow it"), and though she never lived in a polygamous relationship, she was an unwitting product of the polygamous lifestyle.

Sherrie was born into the Fundamentalist Church of Jesus Christ of Latter-day Saints (FLDS) community in Colorado City, Arizona, and Hildale, Utah. "Just because polygamy wasn't lived by my parents doesn't mean I wasn't affected by it," she says. "The belief structure supporting and surrounding polygamy controls, forms and dominates people in every aspect of their lives."

Her father had been a Mormon who followed relatives into FLDS, where he was instructed by the leader to marry Sherrie's mother. "My parents didn't know one another; they only knew each other's names," says Sherrie. "People are taught they are putting complete faith and trust in God when they marry and that the prophet speaks for God."

Sherrie was the eldest of 11 children and, as such, became the confidante of her mother, who constantly told her of the hatred she felt toward Sherrie's father. "My mother was raped by my father countless times and went to the prophet about it," she says. "The prophet is looked upon as the one and only man who can receive the word of God. He told her to do what her 'priesthood head,' my father, told her and there wouldn't be a problem."

Trapped in her own hell, her mother's hatred and powerlessness took an ugly twist. "She took her hatred out on me and my siblings. I lived in terror seeing her throw the babies on the floor, knocking the breath out of them. She beat us, threw things at us and taught us to pray for our father's death," says Sherrie. "She would get our father to beat us when she couldn't get us to do what she wanted; when he reached the point of rage and we were getting hurt really bad, she would stop him and get hurt in the process. Then we had to take care of her."

In one beating from her father, Sherrie was kicked and then thrown across the room. "I hit my head where the barrette was in my hair. It split my scalp and I had blood running down my face. I looked at my mother and she was watching with a smile," says Sherrie. "Later on she stopped him and berated him. It was her way of proving he was nothing."

In addition to the physical abuse, sexual abuse was a daily part of childhood. Sherrie remembers being molested by a man in the FLDS church who was a family friend and by both of her parents. "My father began raping me when I was eight years old. My mother sexually abused all of us, taking us one at a time in her room and telling us it was for medical reasons."

By the time Sherrie was four, she was washing dishes from the seat of a highchair, making meals and caring for a younger sibling. By second grade, she was making six loaves of bread each week. "I never felt like a kid. There was no time to play," she says. "I raised six of my siblings."

Like most families in this enclave, Sherrie's family lived on food stamps, which were often traded for cash to buy other things. The children would gather pig weed from the Utah desert to supplement their diet. Living in a trailer and a tiny house next door, Sherrie's mother would let the children bathe only once a week to save on the water bill.

In school, Sherrie's teachers, the principal and the superintendent were all members of the FLDS church and limited her education to their world view of select topics. Most girls in the area attend school only until they're 13, but Sherrie didn't drop out until midway through the ninth grade when she had to leave to help her pregnant mother at home. She returned to school and had to repeat ninth grade, but dropped out a second time when her mother again became pregnant. "When I turned 16, I got my [high school equivalency degree] and asked the prophet if I could go to college," remembers Sherrie. "He said I couldn't go because I had to stay home and help my mother."

The beatings by Sherrie's father were escalating in violence; and Sherrie confided in a friend, who told her she could call the police. "Mom called the police in town who are all members of the FLDS church. So they came over and pulled my father aside to have a talk with him," says Sherrie. "We stood out there waiting to see what would happen, and my dad and the police started laughing. They walked over to us and told my mom if she'd be obedient, the kids would be obedient and no one would need discipline."

Finally, Sherrie's sister received another beating in which her father kicked her so hard he broke his toe. Her grandmother called the police in another town. "They took us to a safe house for a few days and then sent us back. I don't know what conversations they had with my mother, but I wish they would have asked me about our abuse," she says. "While we were there, the FLDS leaders got word to us to have as little contact as possible with anyone."

Soon after their return, Sherrie's mother and father were granted a divorce by the prophet. "Without our father as the priesthood head in the home, we now had to turn to the prophet for all decisions," she says. "And my father was taken care of by the community."

Sherrie watched her friends, one by one, marry as polygamist wives, live on food stamps and bear children.

Many children in this community come into the world with birth defects due to intermarriage. Some of these deformed babies mysteriously become "poofers," meaning they simply disappear. Down Syndrome, however, is something that is hoped for by expectant parents due to their belief that people with Down Syndrome are compliant and due to the $500 per month government assistance they bring to the community. It is common for mothers to stroke their pregnant bellies and verbally wish for "a Down's."

At age 17, Sherrie began working at one of the local businesses. "I was supposed to turn the money over to my mom; but she spent it all on herself, so I stopped giving it to her," she remembers. "I bought clothes for the little kids; so she went to my boss and had him give her my checks, which she forged and spent." Sherrie told her boss it was illegal for him to give her checks to her mother. Her boss told her he'd lay her off, so Sherrie threatened him with prosecution. When her boss backed down, Sherrie learned the power of standing up for herself. The experience empowered her to make her own decisions, regardless of the orders of others. Her mother told her not to buy a car, so Sherrie bought a car. She started talking to "apostate" kids from the Second Ward. (The split between the First and Second Wards of the FLDS church years earlier had left the community divided with each side accusing the other of apostasy. "Even talking to a Second Warder is bad," she says.)

After a few weeks of asserting herself, fear and guilt from her religious training kicked in; and Sherrie worked harder than ever to fit in and to make her mother happy. "I repented and felt such shame for the tiniest infractions. I gave up on freedom and gave in to everything," she says. "I tried to make it work. All the time growing up, I was taught to be a plural wife. I could not comprehend living polygamy, but I was willing to accept it for God."

In addition to her job at the local shop, Sherrie was also baby-sitting for a friend who was questioning the FLDS religion. "Things she said made me question; and no matter how hard I tried, I couldn't be good," she says. "Then a friend borrowed my car to sneak out to see a boy-friend, and I got fired and kicked out of the house."

With no place to go, Sherrie lived in her car and showered under a waterfall in the red rock canyon narrows. When the weather began turn-ing to winter, she stayed with her grandmother. "That lasted until the bishop told my relatives not to let me live with them or my grandma, or the church would take grandma's house."

Forced back to her mother's house, Sherrie survived by throwing herself into cleaning the yard, burning down an old chicken coop, put-ting in turf and remodeling the trailer. Her mother followed her every-where she went, including the bathroom, writing down every move she made. "Mom wanted me to stay in my room and not talk to my siblings because she was afraid I'd influence them." Sherrie was then confronted by the prophet, who told her she would have to get along with her mother before she could get married. "I was afraid he'd make us marry the same man," says Sherrie. "As far back as I can remember, I thought about suicide. I always thought about suicide. I knew I'd have to leave or kill myself. I couldn't survive there."

The woman she had previously baby-sat for provided the way out. "Her mother had escaped six years earlier, and she told me that her mom would let me live with her until I was on my feet," remembers Sherrie.

"So we devised a plan for the next day when my mother was planning to be out of town."

Sherrie packed a few clothes in garbage bags and walked across a certain bridge with the "garbage" at exactly 2:30 p.m. On December 14th, 1994, at 20 years old, Sherrie caught a ride to freedom. "I knew my mother would think I should just kill myself and get it over with or wish that I hadn't been born, but I left a note in my closet telling her not to worry," she says. "And I told her that now I wouldn't have to be a burden."

Having always worn dresses to her ankles and wrists, the transition into the outside world wasn't easy; and Sherrie found herself feeling depressed. "You feel like you're from Mars," she says. "It was uncomfortable wearing shirts up to my elbows and pants." But she remembered what another refugee had once told her. "He said it would be hard, but not to go back for at least a year. He said to give it time and then I'd see things clearly and be glad I left." Clinging to those words kept her from returning.

After living with her friend's mother for a year and a half, Sherrie moved to Utah Valley and began working in a bronze sculpting business. Utah Valley is home to Brigham Young University and boasts a population that is nearly 100% Mormon. "There was pressure there to join the Mormon Church, and I thought about it because I still partially believed in the FLDS religion," she says. "It was the familiar doctrine without the polygamy; and my family could accept me being a Mormon, though they don't believe it's the 'fullness' of the gospel."

Sherrie was told she had to talk with an LDS general authority about becoming a member of the Mormon Church because she had belonged to the FLDS church. "I spoke with Elder Wirthlin, who said I could be baptized and told me to come back in one year," she says. But Mormonism's continued belief in polygamy proved to be too uncomfortable. "I was baptized; but in six months, I was out of the Mormon Church," she says. "When I asked about polygamy, they said my answers would come in time."

Sherrie went back to visit her mother and siblings and to retrieve the belongings she had left behind. "My mother had given everything away," she says. "My little brother cried and asked why I left and why I didn't care about them anymore." Her mother told her she was evil and was desecrating the house.

She returned once more—to get her W-2 slips so she could apply for financial aid to go to college. Three years later, Sherrie got a levy on her wages to pay the IRS for past taxes. "I never knew you had to file taxes every year. My mother had filed for some of those years and claimed me as head of the house with all my siblings as dependents," she says. "She took the refunds and cashed them. I'm going to prosecute her. I'm standing up for myself."

Sherrie continues to work in bronze sculpting and is planning to buy a home. At 26, she continues to find that the world holds infinite possibilities for her future. And she wears her favorite color, red, the color the FLDS reserves for Jesus alone. "Three years after I left, I needed a dress for an event and went shopping. I found a red dress. All red. Bright red," she laughs. "Red is my favorite color, so I bought it."

15.

Drama In Two Acts

I dim
I dim
I have no doubt
If someone blew
I would go out.

I did not.
I must be brighter than I thought.
—Carol Lynn Pearson, from *Picture Window*

LEONA

In the late 1960s, Elizabeth Code was young, single, staunchly Catholic
and pregnant. Her obstetrician continuously pressured her throughout
the pregnancy to give her child up for adoption. In spite of her situation,
when her infant daughter was born, Elizabeth was hesitant to sign the
consent papers. Lying in the hospital before making up her mind, she
watched as a nurse brought a crying baby to her door only to be admonished by another nurse not to let the mother see the baby. Without seeing her daughter, she eventually gave in to the doctor's persuasion—but
only after he told her that the infant would be adopted by a loving Catholic
couple.

Three months before Elizabeth died at the age of 53, her daughter,
Leona Bull, found her. In what would amount to only a season, the two
would do their best to make up for lost time and to fill in many missing
blanks for one another.

Leona had not been adopted into the home of a loving Catholic couple after all. Not even close. Instead, from what she has pieced together, she believes she was sold on a baby black market to a Mormon fundamentalist polygamist couple.

The adoptive parents, Jack and Darlene Knudson, were wealthy Salt Lake City Mormons who had recently joined the Fundamentalist Church of Jesus Christ of Latter-day Saints based in Colorado City and Hildale in order to live what they considered a more authentic Mormon life. The Knudsons retained their fortune in a religious group that generally believes members must turn over all personal wealth to the church. They owed their special exemption to the church's belief that such wealth is a sign that God has blessed certain individuals to a greater degree than others. The Knudsons were not exempt from paying a large tithe to the church, however.

While living in the Arizona-Utah border town, Jack and Darlene had one natural son before a car accident left Jack paralyzed and in a wheelchair. No longer able to procreate, the Knudsons adopted three daughters, including Leona, from New Mexico within a six year period. Leona would discover years later that in each adoption they used the same doctor and attorney in New Mexico.

The son stayed behind in Colorado City while the parents and daughters moved back to the Salt Lake City area, where Jack maintained the lucrative family businesses. "We visited Colorado City all the time, and that's where our brother was. He never lived with us because Jack and Darlene kept him in Colorado City with the Jessop family," says Leona. "He went to school there, and my sisters and I grew up going to school in the Jeffs compound in Sandy, Utah, until we were 13. Then we were pulled out to work in the family-owned businesses."

What passed as education amounted to home-schooling taught by polygamous women who had themselves been pulled out of inadequate home-schooling by age 13. Leona remembers having one study period and only four subjects taught, including a religion class. "I remember Warren Jeffs ripping pages out of books," she says. "One time he ripped out pages that discussed astronauts walking on the moon. He said the moon landing was all staged in Hollywood."

Eventually, Jack married two more women. "They were women whose husbands had died, and so suddenly our home was full of all these people," Leona says. "We had 36 children in the family, and I went from having my own room to sharing it with five other girls." According to Leona, the expanded household was a place where people simply learned to tolerate one another and their situation. "It was far from being a happy home," she says. "The second wife was mentally handicapped and became the maid, doing all the cooking and cleaning; the third wife was just kind of there."

Darlene was a woman who ruled with an iron fist, and her best efforts went to making her adopted daughters conform to the religion. When the oldest sister, Cathy, rebelled by cutting her long hair, Leona watched in terror, fearing Cathy would drown as Darlene held her under water as punishment. "One time she beat our youngest sister in the bedroom while we sat in another room listening to her screaming. Then it went quiet," remembers Leona. "When Darlene came out, she had all our sheets in her arms and they were covered with blood. We didn't know if Chris was dead or alive." Chris, now grown and away from her adoptive parents, struggles with substance abuse, Leona says.

Though confined to a wheelchair, Jack sexually abused Leona and Chris with his fingers and allowed his business associates to rape them. "One time he was sexually abusing me and Darlene walked into the room," says Leona. "Her eyes met mine and she turned and walked out. She didn't do a thing."

Leona was taught by her religion that, as a woman, her only purpose in life was to have children. By age 15, Leona's brother Robert asked their father if he could marry her. She told her father he'd never see her again if she was forced to marry her brother. Instead, she asked if she could marry a boy from Colorado City who was 19. "The idea of marrying my brother made me sick, and I didn't want to have the council marry me off to an old man," she says. "Another factor was that I wanted out of that house. I didn't get married for love."

Leona didn't get far. The young couple didn't have any money and was forced to move in with her family, where they would remain for a year and a half before moving to a house next door. "My husband never married any other wives," she explains. "He and I were just doing the basics of the religion." Before she reached her 16th birthday, Leona was pregnant. By the time she was 17, she had another child; and her last was born when she was 19.

Just before, during and after each birth, Leona stayed in the leader's home in his walled compound. "I heard the fighting, yelling and screaming from those wives. The prophet's home is where 'celestial marriage' is supposedly lived perfectly," she laughs. "There were young wives who were ostracized from entire sections of the home by the older wives."

As a houseguest, Leona was able to attend one of the prophet's many weddings. "It was right after he had a stroke," she says. "He was marrying a couple of teenage girls from the Steed family, and he had to be held up and reminded of what his name was." By 2000, Rulon Jeffs, age 90, had an estimated 60 wives.

After the birth of her first baby, Leona was horrified to wake up and find her mother-in-law trying to nurse the infant. "After that, my baby wouldn't nurse from me," says Leona. "I had to put her on the bottle." But with a bottle, the baby began vomiting and quickly lost six pounds. "My husband and I had to sneak away to a doctor. Oh, what we had to go through to sneak off," remembers Leona. "The doctor said if we hadn't brought her in when we did, she would have died." They found that their daughter was allergic to milk and had thrush, for which she was prescribed antibiotics. Back at the Jeffs compound, Leona was caught putting the antibiotic drops in her baby's mouth. "They were screaming about me poisoning my baby," she says. "It's a scandal to go to the doctor because you're supposed to pray or have the laying on of hands for a healing blessing. If you don't get better, you don't have enough faith."

Like most members of the religion living in Salt Lake, Leona and her husband and children spent much of their time in Colorado City. During her stays in the community, Leona saw and heard of many tragedies that continue to haunt her. People, mostly "rebellious" children, suddenly die or disappear. Rebellious girls are usually taken to the community's settlement in Canada and married off to older men. For boys, it's another story. "People will be told that this one or that one drowned in the creek. Boys who knew how to swim. Boys they were having trouble with," she says. "They told us one boy suffocated from car exhaust after pulling over to the side of the road for a nap. Another one was supposed to have been hit by a semi truck while crossing the highway because he didn't see it coming." In the Colorado City-Hildale community, the mayors and the police are all members of the group. Suspicious deaths are never questioned, much less investigated.

Eventually, with the decline of Jack's health, the Knudsons decided to sell their home and businesses in the Salt Lake area and move back to Colorado City. Leona and her husband were expected to move with the rest of the family. The couple, however, had been wanting to break with the group and saw this as their chance. "I wanted my kids to have what I never could," says Leona. "An education and just the simple things in life. Like normal clothes."

Not making the exodus with the family was bad enough, but denouncing the religion was considered an unforgivable sin. "It was the hardest decision we ever made. You are physically sick and scared. You don't know how to go into the world without an education," she says. "We had no money, no jobs and three kids. Even now I can't help my own kids with their homework."

By design, the families on both sides made their transition even harder. "We were screamed at, and my husband was told he was a 'Son of Perdition.' They told us we'd fall flat on our faces and come crawling back to them," Leona says. "Now they tell our kids that we're taking them to hell. I heard Darlene tell my oldest daughter that I was working directly against God."

Before the couple left the group, Leona's oldest daughter, who had gone as far as third grade at the Jeffs compound, was put into a daycare run by the group's members. There, according to Leona, she was sexually abused. "On top of that, Darlene conspired with the daycare to take my daughter down to Colorado City, baptize her in the religion and marry her off before we could catch up to them. But we found out and prevented it," she says. "Today she's 17; but after her early schooling and Darlene's influence, I'm still not sure my daughter is totally un-brainwashed. She's getting involved with the Mormon Church because she says it sounds familiar."

In Colorado City, Jack's health continued to deteriorate without a doctor's care. "Darlene put him on herbs and gave him soup for a ruptured appendix," says Leona. "She told me that if God wants him to die, then he'll die." Leona recalls the moment when Darlene wheeled Jack into the council in his frail condition and made him confess to the sexual abuse of his daughters. "Why didn't she do anything when it was happening to us?" she asks rhetorically. "Anyway, all the council did was rebaptize him to wash away his sins." Leona says that after Jack's death, Darlene turned what was left of his fortune over to the church and began living on social security.

After the funeral, one of Jack's other wives handed Leona an envelope. Inside she discovered information about her birth. That information was all she needed to find her birth mother, Elizabeth. "I found her, called her and flew to Albuquerque the next day," she says. "We hugged and cried." After the joy of their reunion, Elizabeth broke down when she heard what kind of life her daughter had been living. "It was horrible for her to find out," say Leona. "And when she saw the papers it was even worse." The women discovered that the dates on the papers, were wrong. The birth certificates were done illegally, and the Utah State Child Welfare Department had done an illegal home inspection since the Knudsons were living in Colorado City, Arizona, at the time. Leona has also learned that the attorney who handled the adoptions of her and her sisters became a judge in New Mexico, had bar sanctions filed against him and had retired. He has refused to talk to Leona and her sister Cathy or Cathy's birth mother about his involvement in the adoptions. The doctor is now dead.

Leona finds a bitter sweetness in the short time she had with her mother and feels grateful that her mother had closure on that chapter of her life. Leona's marriage ended. She is happily living a far different life than the one she was raised to live. "I have within myself what I believe, and I don't need somebody telling me to pay tithing and go to church," she says. "And I believe that people should not be able to adopt babies into polygamous cults."

16

Slaughter of the Innocent

Young and beautiful
Lock her away.
Feast upon her heart,
Rend her soul.
Whisper things to her
That will turn her stomach.
Call her whore
And ingrate.
Tell her she doesn't matter.
She was nobody.
Feed her a bone
And give her flesh to the dogs.
She means nothing to you.
She is not a person.
She is a means to an end.
You will use her
Until you decide she is unworthy.
Discard with the trash,
That's all she is to you.
She was youth and beauty
And now she's dead.
                    —Wendy Worthington

WENDY

Wendy didn't die, as her poem would suggest. At least not literally. But coming out of the intense pain she once suffered changed her so much that the person she once was is gone. In that sense, she did experience a kind of death.

Born to Mormon parents who became disaffected with their church over its abandonment of polygamy and acceptance of blacks into the Mormon priesthood, Wendy's family gravitated toward fundamentalism. By age nine, Wendy was being ushered into the Apostolic United Brethren church with her parents. Two years after joining, a split in that church occurred over leadership succession, and the family sided with the splinter group led by Gerald Peterson.

By the time Wendy was 14, she was well indoctrinated into Peterson's church, The Righteous Branch, which held meetings in a house in St. George, Utah, until it grew to include approximately 100 members scattered throughout Utah and Nevada. The group later built a temple on a hill near Cedar City, Utah, where more space could accommodate the larger membership.

By the age of 17, she was rebelling against the church's teachings and her parents' rules and considering moving in with a "gentile" man she'd been seeing, who was 27. At the same time, Ken Reen, a man who was in charge of the church's youth council, became ill; Wendy's mother arranged for Wendy to move in with his family through the ruse of them needing her help. It was her mother's solution to Wendy's restlessness— allowing her to leave her parents' home, yet keep her safely in the church.

Living in the home of a man who wasn't a father figure or brother figure, Wendy soon found herself developing a crush on Ken. By the time the church was due for its seasonal conference, she decided she would seek direction from the priesthood by asking the prophet to give her a blessing. The prophet asked Ken to assist in the ritual. With their hands on her bowed head, Wendy sat listening to the prophet's words, which led her to think Ken was to become her husband. "He said something about being 'saved by the man who assists you.' So my mother and I thought it was a witness to marry Ken," she says. "The next step was to notify Ken and his wife, Anita, that I was to be in their family." Ken and Anita then had a conversation with her about how best to handle the situation. The couple, who were married the same year Wendy was born, had not yet made a final decision and felt that if they agreed to the marriage, they wanted to keep it secret from their children. "Anita was having problems with it, but said she loved me too much to let me go," she says. "So we decided to do it sooner than later, before we backed out."

With Wendy dressed in a white "temple-regulated" dress, she married Ken in his cousin's family room in Provo, Utah. She remembers hyperventilating during most of the ceremony, which her father officiated. As for wedding pictures, there would be none of Wendy and Ken standing together during or after vows. "We had pictures taken separately because of the paranoia in the church of anyone finding out we lived polygamy," says Wendy. "After our vows, he kissed me on the cheek because his daughter was there."

Later the newlyweds opened presents at a party in their honor, but Wendy sat apart from her new husband and sister-wife. "I wanted to sit by him like Anita was, but they made me move so their daughter could sit by him." This distancing was to foreshadow the relationship Wendy would have with her new husband throughout their marriage.

At the time of Wendy's marriage, the Righteous Branch taught the Law of Sarah, a belief that the biblical Sarah made decisions as to Abraham's relations with his concubine, Hagar. In keeping with that belief, Anita was to decide when and if Wendy would spend time with Ken. While living in the home before the marriage, Wendy had been able to sit next to Ken; now, as his second wife, she was told to sit opposite him. "On our wedding night, he gave me a squeeze and I slept on the floor of the living room on a mat," says Wendy. "I knew I wasn't going to be an equal, but I thought I'd have equal time and a voice in the marriage."

As a healthy woman with needs and desires, Wendy found her marriage far from fulfilling. For the first month, Ken would simply tell her good night before going off to bed. After the first month of living as his second wife, she was kissed. Then for two weeks he slept with her, but would only go so far as to kiss her. Such increasing sexual frustration only became more and more deeply personalized and painful, wounding her in the most profound sense.

"One night Anita and Ken called me into their room to discuss giving us all two weeks in which to rethink the decision of me being a wife," says Wendy. "Anita was struggling with it, so the new rules now had me completely cut off from him. I wasn't even allowed to sit and talk with him."

Devastated by the latest development, Wendy went outside to be alone and cried. After the family went to bed, she came back in the house and went to her room. "Ken knocked on my door, and I thought he might be coming to me one last time; instead, he ripped me to shreds," she says. "He said I was selfish and should be on my best behavior so that Anita would want me in the family. I was to put on my happy face, help her out and not have contact with him without her approval."

Left on her own to become more perfect, Wendy began working at a job near their residence in Provo, Utah. Every week, she would turn her paycheck over to Ken, who would then cash it and give her $10 to purchase everything she needed or wanted for a week.

One late night after work, she asked the manager for a ride home. Instead of going straight home, they detoured to a movie, where he tried to kiss her. She confessed the encounter to Ken, who made her quit her job. The manager's unwanted advance was "her" only major slip-up in a two-week effort of trying to fit Ken's impossible ideal while walking on egg shells.

After the two weeks were up, Ken and Anita decided to move ahead with the marriage arrangement as long as Wendy's nights with Ken would be strictly Anita's decision. "I'd hope it was my night all the time, always wondering, 'Is tonight my night? Is tonight my night? Is tonight my night?'" remembers Wendy. "I was frustrated our marriage wasn't consummated and I'd talk to anyone who would listen. One of Ken's cousins and I would talk all the time about how our lives sucked."

By the time the next church conference was scheduled, Anita had found out about Wendy's manager having tried to kiss her. "So I was told I couldn't go up on the sacred hill where the temple is because of what I'd done," says Wendy. "But then I got a blessing of forgiveness and went to conference, where the adult meeting was having a talk about how a marriage isn't a marriage unless there's consummation."

Soon after that conference, Anita came to Wendy before going to bed and told her that Ken would be coming in at 5 a.m. "As the fire chief of the Provo Fire Department, his schedule had him coming home then. I didn't sleep all night in anticipation," says Wendy. "That morning, he came in, raised his 'arm to the square' [see glossary] and dedicated the room. He stripped down to his garments, prayed and it was done. Then he went back to Anita's room."

For the first hour after Ken left her room, Wendy says she felt good. The long awaited consummation had finally happened. Then, as the sterile nature of the act sunk in, she was flooded with anguish. "He didn't kiss me; he didn't work up to anything; he didn't prepare me for it and it was physically painful," she remembers. "I went in to talk to them, and Anita yelled at me saying she'd given me a beautiful gift and I'd thrown it back in her face." Wendy fell on her knees begging them for forgiveness for her ingratitude.

Feeling the need to visit her family, she drove to Southern Utah for a few days. Once there, she visited with the leader's first wife, Faye. "In my mind, having a baby was the reason for plural marriage; Faye said I was right to want to have children and they were wrong to not let me try to have them," says Wendy. "When I told Ken and Anita what she said, they got mad and yelled at me; but I couldn't give up. I took eternal vows."

The stress and unhappiness were taking their toll on Wendy. She began falling into a depression and was unable to eat. There were fights about not eating, fights about moving her to another bedroom and fights about moving her things while she was away from the house. Finally, Ken told Wendy the family was falling apart, and that the only way to fix it would be for her to move out. He then called the church prophet and asked if she could be released from their eight-month marriage. "After he got permission from the prophet, Ken raised his hand to the square and released me," says Wendy. "I cried and cried, then walked outside and collapsed."

After returning to her family in Southern Utah, she attempted a polygamous marriage one more time by marrying her sister's husband for one week. "I had gone into my marriage with Ken with a sister-wife mindset, so I thought, 'Here is my real sister who I love and she loves me, so this has got to work,'" she says. "But I just couldn't do it. I left."

Wendy left Utah, moving to New York to work as a nanny for a year and then relocating to Las Vegas, Nevada. "A year and a half later, I wrote Ken and Anita a letter trying to get closure and to see if they would admit that it was wrong what they did to me. They didn't, and they never will," she says. "As far as polygamy goes, it never works out.

It's first and foremost a way to subjugate women. No woman can have any worth because value is dictated by the husband, so [she has no inherent] value."

In Las Vegas, Wendy continued to struggle with pain she couldn't comprehend by self-mutilating, punching walls and engaging in risky behavior, such as accepting rides with strangers.

One spring evening, Wendy left a casino with a man who said he was just going to walk her to her car. He instead forced her to drive into the mountains. Wendy struggled, and he began choking her. He raped her; then had her drive him back to Las Vegas, where he got out of the car and disappeared. She reported the assault to police, but the assailant was never apprehended. Through Nevada's reparations program for victims of violent crime, she was (and still is) provided with therapy. "The assault was easy compared to being married," she says. "I went to therapy and said, 'The rape isn't what I want to talk about. I've got this other (situation) to deal with.' Now I'm trying to get closure."

Wendy has now been out of polygamy for eight years and says she looks at her experience in terms of seeing herself as a different person.

"There is no connection to who I was then and who I am now," she says. " It makes it easier to say it's not me they did it to."

17.

Just ten days ago Hyrum brought home
A new wife. My heart is rather heavy.
   —Ellen Clawson, Letter to Ellen Pratt
   McGary, 1856

TAMMY

It didn't take long for Tammy Steeves to hitch a ride to the airport. At 17, pretty, blond and petite, a ride was the least of her problems that summer. With just $320 in her pocket, she could only hope it would be enough to get her to San Francisco. Once there, she planned on reuniting with the mother who left her and five other daughters with their father when Tammy was a baby.

Growing up on a picturesque Indiana farm with her father, stepmother and nine other children was far from the ideal it might seem. More than running toward her estranged mother, she was actually running from a brutally abusive and loveless childhood. By the time Tammy made it to San Francisco, she had $20 left.

She finished high school in California while living with her mother and her mother's fifth husband. After graduation, she moved in with her boyfriend. "Don was good looking and into drugs. Not the settle-down type," she says. "When I had my baby, he just couldn't handle it and we split up."

On the rebound, she married again. By the time she was eight-months' pregnant with a third child, her second husband was gone. "He left me with three children and thousands of dollars of unpaid bills and fines," she remembers. "Then I was served with a warrant for welfare fraud because I was using welfare and hadn't reported his income, which he had never used for me and the children."

To settle the charges with the California welfare department, she served a sentence under house arrest, wearing an ankle band and paying off the debt by getting a loan. "That got me back in school and into the work force, so it ended up being a good thing," she says.

With her friend, Heather, Tammy began attending the Mormon Church, which helped her with food. "My first home teacher in the church gave me a job," she said. "But then he fell in love with me and told his wife. So the church moved me to a different ward."

Going to Mormon Church-sponsored dances for single adults in the Sacramento area became a good avenue for Tammy to help another Mormon friend, who was an invalid, get out of the house. "Those dances were a meat market; every new woman caused a stampede. One time I walked in, and guys literally knocked over a food table to get to me," she says. "I wanted to stay single, but it was good to help my friend. I suck up other people's problems so I don't have to deal with my own."

Finally one night at a church dance, Tammy met a shy man who told her his name was Michael Alexander. "He was very good-looking and wore a three-piece suit," she says. "He told me he was a bishop in Redding and was divorced with seven children. When he asked for my phone number, I gave it to him."

From April through July, Michael called Tammy every night, talking until three or four in the morning, starting each conversation by asking her if she had said her prayers and inquiring about what scripture she had read last. He would send Mormon Church history books for her to read, all of which dealt with polygamy in the early church. "Then on the phone one night, we started reading *Doctrine and Covenants* Section 132 together," she says. "He said that he still saw his wife and still cared about her, but they split because she reached such a spiritual plane where she no longer needed sex."

Insinuating himself further into Tammy's life, he began having phone conversations with her children and asking what contact their fathers had in their lives. "I was sad that after my third child, I could no longer have any more children; and he told me that with the power of the priesthood he could heal me to have more, like Sarah in the Bible," says Tammy. "After over a month of telephone courtship, he came by for the first time. I felt like I knew him and so did my kids."

When Michael came to dinner, he brought more with him than gifts of flowers, candy and honey. He also brought along a wife. "We had dinner and then read scriptures together," recalls Tammy.

Tammy was bothered by his undefined marital situation and phoned him the next day with questions. He explained that he and his wife lived in the same house, but were basically separated. When Tammy asked what his wife thought about him courting her, he said that his wife and children had all dreamed of Tammy. "He said that I was the fulfillment of prophecy and of his personal revelation and was sent to them," she says. "I felt chosen and special. All this coming from a man who seemed to never have anything but a spiritual thought."

And then the wife, Sylvia, came to visit by herself. "She had a four-month-old baby and she came in and said, 'Do you know how long we've been waiting and looking for you?'" says Tammy. "She was pleasant and humble, and I held the baby while we talked. She told me I was to have more babies."

Sylvia confided to Tammy that Michael's real name was Luis Gonzales, but that he used an alias so that women he courted could call and the other wives would instantly know what the call was about. Sylvia painted a beautiful picture of happy wives baking bread and spending long hours nurturing children in their home school with no corrupting television allowed. "It sounded like a good way to raise children and live a purposeful life," says Tammy. "They kept coming over and bonding, and I believed them when they said they were sent to teach me."

Before long, Tammy was included in a study group with 40 other adults from surrounding Mormon wards who had secretly aligned themselves with Luis and his Church of Jesus Christ of the United Order. "The study group members called him 'bishop,' paid him tithing, and donated money, a house and cars for his use. We all took an oath of secrecy," she says. "And then I met the other wife, Frances. But I still felt okay because she had a baby. There were all these babies and, it seemed, so much love."

In this religion of roughly 200 members, half of the group live in Daviess County, Missouri, near a place known by Mormons and Mormon polygamist fundamentalists as Adam-Ondi-Ahman (see glossary). The other half of the members remain in the Sacramento, California, area where they live the pretense of being mainstream Mormons. Mormon Church members, in general, are a tight-knit community. Entrance to Mormon temples requires a "Temple Recommend" given only to mainstream Mormons who pay tithing to the Mormon Church. Unknown to Mormon Church leaders, some members of Luis's church print their own temple recommends to get into the Mormon Temple. Others are well known Mormons leading what appear to be mainstream Mormon lives and attending temple sessions with official Mormon recommends; while others, including some who are on Mormon Church Stake High Councils, are well situated in the local Mormon community to have easy access to Mormon temples.

In the Church of Jesus Christ of the United Order, a man must have three wives to be elevated to the highest degree of glory. Additional wives are an extra benefit. "They go to regular Mormon Church with only one of the wives. If someone asks questions about another wife, they say she's a sister," explains Tammy. "I thought it was about serving God and not about sex at all."

After several months, Tammy told her friend Heather that she was going to marry Luis. Leaders from Missouri came to interview her about whether former husbands would be involved with the children. She also had to have a special swearing in to the church before she could marry Luis because she wasn't a virgin. "We were married on the fourth of July, but it was more about commitment to the group than a marriage," she says. "Frances cried the whole time, and Luis had to spend our honeymoon with her because she was so upset."

The religion teaches that no one should use checks or credit cards due to the "mark of the beast." (This includes not just 666 but the "seeing eye" on dollar bills.) They also refuse to get driver's licenses and birth certificates for their children or pay taxes. "They taught that it was all Satan's way of keeping you from multiplying and replenishing the earth," says Tammy. "But I still kept my driver's license. They said that once we all moved to Missouri, we'd put pressure on the local government to outlaw driver's licenses."

Tammy felt fairly secure in her new marriage, with a rental house, children and a man who wasn't always "on top of me." She had an extended family that included 15 children and two sister-wives whom she considered good friends. She was feeling lucky.

Luis began planning a trip to Utah to visit with other Mormon fundamentalist polygamists and decided Tammy should accompany him since they would use her driver's license to rent a car. "Luis was to go to Utah and get books written by Ogden Kraut to translate them into Spanish so the polygamists could use them to convert girls in Mexico," says Tammy. "They like how the girls there have a culture that teaches them to be compliant to men."

After Tammy and Luis returned to California from Utah, she found that her house was now occupied by 22, including Luis's other two wives. "They gutted it, tore out the cabinets and threw away all my belongings," she says. "They had food storage stacked up everywhere and folded beds and mats for sleeping. That was it."

Tammy was told that this was part of being in the group. In addition, she would have to live by new rules to free her from her selfishness. She could no longer continue to hold her present job; instead, she would have to work for Luis. She could no longer wear makeup or her sexy underwear, and her kids could only have three changes of clothes each. "Then they made me watch a movie called *The Devil's Advocate*," she says. "I was supposed to identify with a woman in the movie who goes crazy and kills herself because she won't submit to her husband."

At night, when Tammy lay on her mat trying to sleep, she left the radio on next to her so she wouldn't have to hear her husband having sex with one of his other wives. "It didn't work, so I started taking an herb that Sylvia recommended to knock me out," she says. "Then I'd wake up; and people would tell me that I was levitating, speaking in tongues in a man's voice and acting possessed. After that I was afraid to sleep."

As sleep deprivation progressed, and as Sylvia gave her one herbal remedy after another, Tammy began feeling afraid to be anywhere without Luis. "There were no labels. I don't know what I was taking, but I felt strange."

Three months later, Tammy suffered an especially painful menstrual period. "They told me they had a revelation that I had been pregnant;

but, because I wasn't submissive enough, I had let an evil spirit in and miscarried. This reinforced my inability to be alone. I didn't want to be left by anyone."

In the meantime, Tammy's oldest daughter was struggling with the new polygamous lifestyle. She wanted out and decided to move in with a girlfriend. "I couldn't explain to her how I had to be with the group and I couldn't make them leave," says Tammy. "So she moved out, and her friend's mother called California's Child Protective Services (CPS)."

Tammy told the CPS worker that she was Sylvia's half-sister, that Sylvia was married to Luis and that Frances was Luis's sister and everyone was in a business together. "That was our routine for the outside, so that's what we told this woman from CPS," says Tammy. "After she left, Luis said something bad would happen to her for showing up like that; two weeks later, she fell on some stairs and broke her back. The next CPS worker just pushed our case aside."

No one had been paying the rent or utility bills on the house, so Luis insisted that the house had to be abandoned. Tammy, however, wanted to maintain her residence. "One night Sylvia gave me an herb and Luis came in and had sex with me. Really rough sex. Then he left, and an hour later came in saying he just arrived," remembers Tammy. "When I explained that he had been with me just an hour before, they said it was an evil spirit that took body form because I was being rebellious about the house."

Convinced they were right and more afraid than ever, Tammy packed up and moved with the others. Having made the sacrifice of her home, she was now able to participate in an endowment temple ceremony modeled after the Mormon Temple ceremony. "They gave me temple garments and made me do the sign of slashing my throat, just like in the Mormon temple."

The group was still concerned that CPS was on their trail, so they bought a 20-passenger van to move to Missouri. Just as they were about to leave, Luis decided that he and Tammy would stay behind in California. "His other wives got upset, and I said I wouldn't go anywhere without my kids," says Tammy. "He was mad about all the disobedience, so he left us all helpless and without money. He kept all the money."

Tammy's friend Heather wired some money for the purchase of rice and beans. After nearly a month, Luis returned, asking who had pulled things together during his absence. When everyone answered that Tammy had, he announced that it had been a test for others to see why he needed her. Then he took everyone out for Chinese food. "Everyone was so happy to see him; everything was wonderful," she says. "But I was mad. The situation he put us through had been horrible."

The group stayed in California and settled into a four-bedroom house with Luis and his three wives sharing one bedroom. "There we are, him having sex with each wife and each one of us trying to sleep, pretending he's not having sex with the others," says Tammy. "There was huge competition to serve him, to look the way he wanted, fighting over his time. So then came the calendar."

The days of the calendar were marked with each woman's initials. If a woman wasn't sufficiently obedient on the day her initials were marked, her night was given to another woman. "On your night, you got to share in his privileges—go out for ice cream, whatever he did," says Tammy. "If you lost your night, you had to stay up all night and read scriptures."

As the women strived to fit an idealized appearance, Tammy says that Frances began purging and walking around at night. Sylvia went without food for days on end, starving herself into a size three. Then Sylvia and Frances began competing in a race to find a new wife for Luis. "They brought women over behind my back and told me it wasn't proper for me to question," says Tammy. "Then he would go out late at night, saying he was going on appointments. But since I worked for him, I knew he didn't have appointments."

Before Tammy met the latest future sister-wife, she was told that the woman, Antoinette, was dying and needed Luis to take care of her because Luis had produced a child with her many years ago. "When I met her, she didn't know a thing about dying. I had been lied to, so I was hostile," remembers Tammy. "They told me that if I'd been close enough to the Lord, I'd know she was supposed to be part of the family; so they didn't really lie about something I should know and it was my fault for not knowing this."

Tammy decided sharing Luis with yet another woman was the end of what she could endure. She wanted out of the marriage and the religion, but they told her she didn't really want to leave after having taken covenants. "So now I can't leave. I'm not allowed to use the phone or talk to my kids or I might influence them," she says. "They read and read scriptures to me and called a council meeting. Then I'm locked in my room for eight hours with no food."

While Tammy sat in her room trying to think of a way to get out of the situation, she noticed Luis's backpack in the closet. Knowing that he always kept his gun in his backpack, she started concocting a plan. "I was going to go into the council meeting and hold the gun on them, send my kids to the car and demand the car keys so we could get away," she says. "But I had never held a gun before. Luis came in and noticed I'd been in the backpack, so he had the whole group come in and told them I was going to kill myself and they needed to do an exorcism on me."

As emotionally broken down as she was, Tammy couldn't bring herself to tell them what she was really planning to do. She wept during the exorcism, leading the church members to conclude that she was cleansed.

"After sleeping, I woke up still wanting to leave, still not wanting another woman," she says. "So I called Antoinette and we got together. She wanted to know what it was like living polygamy and I told her it was awful. We parted civilly."

The next day, Luis demanded that Tammy come to the office. "I said no, so he came home and grabbed me by the hair and took me to the office. He asked if I talked to Antoinette and I said no, so he hit me and broke my eardrum."

While blood flowed from Tammy's ear to her shoulder, Luis's voice became fuzzy as he told her she was full of evil spirits. Then he raped her, telling her he was giving her what she wanted. After three hours of brutalization, he called his other wives, instructing them to get Tammy's belongings together.

When the sister-wives came, Sylvia cleaned Tammy's ear while Luis drafted papers for her to sign stating that she fell and broke her eardrum. She was also forced to sign her life insurance over to Luis and state that she would give her children and all her belongings to him if anything ever happened to her. "I signed so I could go. Then I called Heather to wire me money. The van was in my name; so they let me take it, and I drove to Heather's," says Tammy. "She wanted me to call the police, but I couldn't because all the guns and ammunition the group stockpiled were in my name. My name was on all his business records; I was party to welfare fraud and the lie to CPS." Once at Heather's house, Tammy received at least ten phone calls a day from Luis telling her that he still loved her.

One morning, Heather read a newspaper article about Tapestry Against Polygamy. Tammy gave them a call. The next day, she and her children were on a train to Utah. They stayed with Tapestry members for nearly two months. Tapestry's attorney, Douglas White, canceled her life insurance and drew up a new will. "Once out of the group, I knew I wasn't possessed and I found out I wasn't alone," she says. "I saw women who had reclaimed their own lives, and I knew for the first time that I could recover."

Tammy returned to California, living in a motor home until she could rent an apartment. She felt she had gained new strength. She wanted to help her former sister-wives learn what she learned from Tapestry and to tell them that they did not have to live the way they were living. "I was drawn back to the women and kids. They were all living at Folsom Lake in tents at a campground, cooking over a [fire pit]," she says. "Sylvia was pregnant, and Frances was due to deliver a baby in three weeks; so I left my motor home for them to live in and took a car they had."

A week after her visit to the group, she received a call from Sylvia, who told her that she would have to come and tell CPS workers that the two women lived at her house or social workers would take the kids and put Luis in jail. Tammy drove back to Folsom Lake and signed a document taking responsibility for the women and children. "Then Luis took off again, leaving me the only one with a car and any money; so I told them I'd stay until he got back," says Tammy. "While he was gone, Frances delivered her baby in a hotel I put her in. Then Luis came back and said he left because of a revelation that we were to be alone to bond with each other."

As the rest of the group began moving into the hotel with Frances, Tammy started looking for a house to rent for herself and her children. "With everyone crowding her out of her hotel room, I offered Frances the chance to stay with me once I got in my own place; but then when the money I put on the hotel room ran out, they all came to my place," she says. "I was right back in the middle of it."

To get out of the situation this time, Tammy moved with her children out of the house she'd rented and into an apartment. "I'm supporting myself and my kids. Working was the only way for me to stay out," she says. "But then Luis started showing up with candy, flowers and cards and saying he's going to tell my boss everything. Then the sister-wives came with cookies."

Tammy begged Luis not to talk to her boss, but he held it over her head so she would accept his gifts and continue to see him. Finally she sat her boss down and told him herself. With her boss no longer providing leverage, Luis began calling her to tell her he had a revelation that men at work would want her for kinky sex. She ignored him. So Luis found out where her kids were going to school and went to see them, where they innocently gave him the new address and home phone number. Tammy didn't answer when he called, so he drove over to her apartment. One night he called to tell her he was in bed with a woman and having sex. A woman got on the line and described how wonderful he was.

Not wanting Frances to get a sexually transmitted disease from Luis, Tammy warned her that he was sleeping with at least one other woman. "So Frances asked him about it. He told her he had another wife, but couldn't share her because of everyone's jealousy," says Tammy. "Eventually they all got together and then they wanted me to meet her." When she met the new wife, Heather, Tammy discovered she was mentally impaired due to an accident and the beneficiary of a settlement.

Luis, Frances, Sylvia and the children then settled into Heather's five-bedroom home with her and her five children. "After they moved out of my house, the kids and I moved back in," says Tammy. "But they hadn't paid the rent for six months, so we were getting evicted. Then they all showed up again just as I was getting evicted; they were homeless."

Tammy found another house to rent, and they all moved in together with everyone pooling their money. "Every time they got in my life, I wound up with nothing but my job," she says. "So my real plan at this point was to move them and take off again on my own with my kids."

Before she was able to find a place to go, she avoided contact with Luis in the shared house. "One Sunday I didn't want to go to church, and it was like a slap to him," Tammy remembers. "He came out to where I was in the garage, sat down with his backpack and started talking." Luis told Tammy that she had to accept him and be happy. He pulled out the scriptures and read and explained how Emma Smith, the first wife of Joseph Smith, was commanded by God to accept polygamy. Then he talked about evil spirits and how he needed to be there to help her the next time they come to her. "He took out his gun and put it on the pillow saying he wouldn't stop me. Then he flipped. He ripped off my clothes and raped me," she says. "I had the feeling he would kill me and make it look like suicide, so I told him what he wanted to hear. After an hour, he finally believed me and I got dressed."

As Tammy was plotting her chance to move with the kids, Luis caught on and asked her if she was going to leave. When she said she was, he grabbed her by the hair, backhanded her and threw her into the nearby bushes. "I got up and went to a pay phone and called the police while Frances drove Luis off to hide," remembers Tammy. "I had a black eye and a cut lip and the police were asking about all the kids." As Tammy tried to talk to the police, her knees buckled and she sank to the floor. They thought she had fainted.

With only the clothes on their backs, Tammy and her children went to a hotel and started over from scratch. Luis would call her at her work as often as 20 times each day and try to meet her for lunch. After she got a car, he stole her registration papers from the glove compartment. When she rented another house, he took mail from her mail box. Restraining orders were met with deliveries of flowers. Children of other wives would be dropped off for visits. Harassing phone calls at home and work continued.

Finally, Luis was arrested after Tammy spotted him from her office window calling her from a phone booth across the street; she phoned the police from another office line. He was out of jail in four days. She then endured phone calls at her home, with Luis telling her that God said it was more righteous for him to destroy her than to let her sin with other men. The police put a trace on her phone that logged 375 phone calls from him in one month, but they failed to do anything until Tammy was able to talk to a female detective. Luis was arrested; and while in jail awaiting a court date, he began calling Tammy's daughter at school. The calls pushed the girl to confide to a teacher that Luis had molested her and had been threatening her.

Luis Gonzales was charged with two felony child abuse charges in addition to violating a restraining order, stalking, bigamy, spousal rape and spousal abuse. As Tammy waited for the day she would face Luis in court, she decided to contact the mainstream Mormon Church, thinking she and her children would return to the faith she once held. The bishop, however, told her to wait. "He said I shouldn't get rebaptized until this all dies down or it could bring bad publicity to the church," she says.

In preliminary court proceedings, Luis claimed religious freedom to practice the patriarchal, hierarchal law as a father, husband and head of the house. He was aided by an attorney with the Utah ACLU in defending the bigamy charges.

In July 2002, Luis was convicted of one count of bigamy, one count of spousal abuse and 20 counts of child molestation. The jury of ten women and two men deadlocked on three counts of spousal rape and one count of stalking. Judge Trena H. Bsurger-Plavan in Sacramento County sentenced him to 59 years and four months in prison.

Tammy is struggling emotionally with issues from her past but working hard at rebuilding her life and providing for herself and her three children. She has since remarried.

18.

Hope is the thing with feathers in my soul
That sings the song without words
And never stops at all.
—Emily Dickinson

SARAH

Maybe someday Sarah will be able to stop looking over her shoulder. Maybe someday the shadows that plague her life will evaporate; but polygamy handed her some very persistent, very ominous shadows.

Sarah's father had been a dedicated Mormon who taught LDS seminary to high school students for ten years. He left his wife and ten children to marry two of his Mormon seminary students (as soon as they graduated from high school) before being excommunicated by his Mormon bishop. One of the students he married was Sarah's mother. "He took his wives out of the city and into Utah's desert, where he married a third woman," says Sarah. "There were eventually 39 of us kids from his three wives."

Utah's desert is unforgiving, with basically two seasons—one of sizzling heat and the other of freezing cold. In the extreme harshness of their environment, the mothers and children labored daily to carve out a life by hauling water, milking cows and growing a garden. Electricity came from a generator, and the children were home-schooled by the mothers. As independent polygamists, they didn't mix with any of the known polygamist groups. Their only visitors were other independent polygamists and survivalist friends who came by on a regular basis. "My father had us isolated to control our lives," says Sarah. "He was strict. I was once spanked for saying, 'cool.'"

As an early developing girl, Sarah began her period by the age of nine. "It was then that my dad started talking to me about marrying a friend of his who I overheard telling my dad that I was a ripe fruit ready to fall off a tree," remembers Sarah. "It got worse when I turned 13 and would have to go on walks with the friend, Lloyd Roper, who was after a third wife. Dad wanted to marry Lloyd's daughter, so they began working on a trade."

Sarah was determined to explore her options; and when one of her father's wives was allowed to move to Salt Lake to begin pre-med studies, Sarah moved with her against her father's wishes. "I wanted to live my own life," she says. "But I was crushed with guilt and uncertainty." The guilt soon returned her to her family in the desert.

A Mormon who had just begun living polygamy had started visiting the family with his young son, bringing high drama to Sarah and her sisters. "We were all going on walks with him," says Sarah. "We all planned on marrying him, and he ate it up."

Instead of marrying each and every sister who wanted him, the young man married only one. When he decided to marry a second wife, his first bride divorced him. "Instead of me, he picked another sister. I was crushed," says Sarah. "I went back to Salt Lake and went to work in a computer shop for a Mormon man who wanted to marry me." The marriage never took place because her boss was unable to convince his wife to accept polygamy. Sarah continued working in the shop, however, and met a customer whom she began dating. "Mack and I were spending a lot of time together and one night we had sex," she says. "So he pronounced us married. Then we said some vows to each other."

The couple lived together in Salt Lake for three months and then moved to Hanna, Utah, where Mack's father, Fred Collier, lived with his polygamist followers in an old Mormon Church. "Fred used to be a member of the LeBaron group in Mexico," says Sarah. "He left them with his wives and started his own religion called The Church of The First Born Lamb of God. We had 76 people living there and it was crowded."

Sarah and Mack lived in their own room in the church; and for six months no one exposed her to the beliefs of the religion, though her husband was pressuring her to become involved. "For my 17th birthday, Mack gave me the book *Women of Mormondom* [Edward Wheelock Tullidge, Tullidge and Crandall, 1877]," she says. "I thought if I didn't become involved in the religion, I was being shallow and self-centered."

She began going to meetings to please Mack. To help her cultivate faith, he and his father would give her blessings, telling her she would become a stronger believer. "It was all very gradual and steady," she says. "Then Mack began pressuring me to get baptized, and I resisted in my typical passive way of not knowing how to say no."

Fred ran a printing press in the church, turning out his own doctrinal materials and pamphlets, and Sarah began working on the press. In addition to operating the printing press, the church members ran a winery. "I was introduced to alcohol and was drinking all the time," she says. "We all drank constantly."

Several new converts moved into the Hanna church from California and Colorado, giving Fred all their money. The new members were going to get baptized, and Sarah decided she would join them. "I got smashing drunk and got baptized, never knowing what they believed until afterward; and then I was inundated with information."

Fred was believed to be the "One Mighty and Strong" and the reincarnated Joseph Smith. Polygamy was practiced by all the men, though Mack still hadn't "taken" another wife. Sarah was learning a new brand of Mormon fundamentalism, but still was not privy to secrets known only to the group's inner circle.

In the meantime, life went on inside what they called the Hanna House. "We had to ask Fred for everything we needed, even to buy shoes. No one had money except Fred," she says. "Life was chaotic. There was no schooling for the children, and we lived on food stamps and Medicaid. The kids were filthy. Freemen and other anti-government friends of Fred's were always in and out."

The group's inner circle held temple ceremonies, and only those who were deemed ready for the higher laws were allowed to attend or know anything about it. "Fred had once worked in the Mormon Church archives and said he had a copy of the undiluted temple ceremony," she says. "One day Mack told me that Fred wanted to take me for a walk."

Sarah went on the walk with her father-in-law and listened as he explained the "Doctrine of Total Commitment." In the doctrine, all men had to be "priesthood adopted" to Fred. All that they owned had to be given to him, including their wives and children. He went on to tell her of the children he had fathered by wives of other men in the group and that Mack also had to give his wife to him. "He said, 'Mack is afraid you won't want to do it,' and then he tried to kiss me," remembers Sarah. "I was crying. I didn't understand how Mack could want to give me to his father. When I got back to Mack, he was crying too and saying he didn't know how he'd do it either; but to be in God's graces he had to."

No matter how she tried, Sarah couldn't bring herself to accept the doctrine and fought with Mack and Fred over it daily. She began learning about all the others who were involved, including some of her best friends in the group. These friends told her how they knew the doctrine was true and important for salvation or they otherwise wouldn't be able to do it. The pressure never let up on her.

To try to gain a testimony (unquestioning belief) of the doctrine, she went on a fast, existing only on water. Throughout her fast, Sarah prayed, read and studied Fred's revelations and the words of Joseph Smith. On the 17th day, after kneeling in prayer, she stood up and instantly fainted. "When I came to, Mack gave me several glasses of wine and a sandwich. I got very drunk and was crying when Fred came in," she remembers. "He said that because I was Mack's wife, technically they didn't need my permission."

Worn to the breaking point physically and emotionally, she confessed to not knowing what else to do. "Mack picked me up and carried me into his father's bedroom, and Fred had sex with me," says Sarah. "When he was done, I went back to my room and cried. I was humiliated and shamed. Mack and I cried together, but I was the one who went through it."

Mack wanted Sarah to consider herself married to his father, who wanted to spend the night with her twice a week and sometimes more. His father began pressuring Mack to marry a second wife and had picked out a 12-year-old girl for him. "Mack asked me to go talk to the girl; but every time I went to talk to her about marriage, she was playing with dolls so I wouldn't," she says. "Then Mack would get mad and blame me saying, 'How can you be married to my dad and yet I can't have another wife?'"

Sarah found herself feeling physically sick again when she was informed that Fred had married his daughter, Ann, as a polygamous wife. Fred's religious doctrine justifies father-daughter incest by teaching that Eve was Adam's child because she was created from his rib and Mary was

God's child. "Ann told me that she threw up when they had sex at first, but she knew she had to do it to be with God," says Sarah. "I used to fantasize about killing Fred myself," she says. Instead, twice while living in Hanna, she tried to commit suicide.

Now as a member of the inner circle, Sarah and the others stood together and raised their hands to the square in sworn oaths never to reveal the principle of total commitment or they would pay through their own blood atonement. Like so many other cult leaders, Fred required nothing less than the ultimate price from his followers. And followers will pay that price gladly when it is cloaked in religion.

The tragic incendiary events in Waco, Texas, began to unfold, causing Fred's survivalist friends to warn him that he too was on a government hit list. "Fred got really paranoid and started stocking up on guns and ammunition and putting people on lookout," says Sarah. "That wasn't enough, so he moved us to Mexico where we stayed in the LeBaron colony."

At this point, Sarah and one of her friends decided they had as much as they could take and needed to leave the group. They hitchhiked with the friend's five children to California. "You could leave, but you couldn't escape from your own head," she says. "Mack and Fred tracked us down, and we went back to Hanna House. With us there, everyone else came back too."

Life in Hanna went on as before for the next nine months until several members left the group, causing Fred to panic. "He got paranoid again; and so we went to Mexico in three vans packed with kids, guns and belongings," she says. "Then we traveled down to the Yucatan, where Fred dumped the guns."

Sarah was sick, not knowing that she was pregnant. The group traveled for months through El Salvador, Nicaragua, Costa Rica and Belize. "We'd be pulled over and be searched by bandits who took our stuff," she says. "I was numb. I would wish they'd just shoot us."

Several times along the way, the group encountered a couple from Canada who took pity on the filthy, unkempt children but were helpless to do anything. Sarah saw an opportunity and secretly asked them if they would take her to the airport in Costa Rica. The couple agreed, and she slipped inside their RV trailer. Once at the airport, she called her sister to wire her some money and borrowed the rest from her Canadian rescuers. She climbed back in the RV to sleep until it was time to board the plane, only to be awakened by Mack and Fred pounding on the RV door. "Fred was threatening to shoot, so I got out and spent the next four hours arguing with them," she says. "Mack was begging and Fred was demanding, so I agreed to extend the ticket a day to talk. We all camped out on the beach while they, and others, argued with me to stay."

That night, as the group was sleeping, Sarah was feeling uneasy about oversleeping and missing her plane. She got out of her blanket and walked along the beach. "Fred was drunk and he came over to me and punched me," she remembers. "Then he raped me, the whole time quoting scriptures; when he finished, he told me I'd burn in hell." Sarah left on the plane that morning.

Three days after arriving in the U.S., she went to a doctor and found out she was pregnant. "My first thought was that I wanted Mack to be with me," she says. "He had called my dad and left a number where he could be reached in Guatemala, so I called. He wanted me to come back."

Sarah asked him to leave his father, but Mack wouldn't do it. "He wouldn't budge, and when I told him about what happened on the beach, he said his dad shouldn't have hit me, but if a husband wants to have sex with his wife, she should be willing," she says. "Then he told me his dad went back to the states, and that he was in Guatemala with three others, so I could come and be with him." She got on a plane and flew back. As Sarah descended from the plane, she found Mack standing next to Fred. She was promised that Fred would be leaving soon. He didn't.

Since they didn't believe in hospitals or doctors, Sarah was soon preparing to have her first baby with a Guatemalan midwife who didn't speak English. After 71 hours of labor, her son was born. Both mother and child were unconscious.

By this time, the group had sold everything they had and were out of money. They needed to get back to Hanna, but Sarah's baby didn't have a birth certificate or passport. After nearly two months, both were finally obtained, and Fred's followers went back to the states on a bus. "I stayed in Hanna with Mack for three more months," says Sarah. "I knew I wanted to leave and I hated myself. The only thing that kept me going was my baby." After packing a few items, she told Mack she was going to take the baby and visit her sister in Salt Lake for a few days. She never went back to Hanna.

Sarah was able to get on food stamps and start school before Mack caught up with her. He moved in with her, but was still unable to cut the ties to his father. By the time he left to go back to Hanna, Sarah was pregnant again.

With two of her sisters living and working in Denver, Sarah decided to move there. Once in Colorado, she got two jobs and continued nursing her baby while pregnant. On three occasions, Fred phoned her and warned her that if she ever told the secrets of his religion, he would kill her through blood atonement and take the children. "And Mack would call and work the religious angle on me," she says. "When I was nine months along, he called me at two in the morning wanting me back and promising to support us. He had never had a job before; he never worked."

The next day, Mack made his way through her front door with promises of being a husband and father. He found a job in construction, bringing home enough money for Sarah to quit one of her jobs. For a brief moment, she thought they might succeed in being a family. "One night Mack had a dream that he was doing the wrong thing," she remembers. "The next day, his dad called and told him that he'd had a revelation that Mack was to serve a mission in Mexico for him. Mack told me, 'I'm leaving now.'"

In desperation, Sarah got on her knees and begged him to stay, telling him that if he left this time, he could never be with her and the children again. Mack shut the door behind him. Sarah delivered a baby daughter the next day.

For a year and a half, Mack spread the word of his father's religion to the people of Mexico, sending converts to Hanna. He sent letters home to Sarah; and after he returned, he begged her to take him back. She refused.

Mack went back to Hanna and after two years and two more failed marriages, he finally left his father's religion to join the Mormon Church. The two only see one another when Mack comes to visit the children. "Even now he won't condemn his father," says Sarah. "Fred had three children with his daughter, Ann, and Mack still won't say his father was wrong."

Sarah had settled into a routine revolving around her children, work and going back to school. Though difficult, her future was taking shape—only to have it come crashing in.

During Utah's investigation into notorious polygamist Tom Green, Juab County prosecutor David Leavitt and Ron Barton, special investigator for the state Attorney General's office, wanted to talk with anyone who knew Green. Sarah had known him when he was briefly "priesthood adopted" to Fred. "He used to brag how he really married Linda Kunz when she was nine years old instead of 13 like everyone was led to believe," remembers Sarah. "He would always say that it's a good thing the gentiles don't know."

Sarah and her sister were interviewed on tape by Leavitt and Barton, who recorded six hours of testimony not only about Green, but long and detailed information concerning Fred Collier and the abuses in his church. At the beginning of the tapes, Sarah and her sister give their names, addresses and phone numbers. "The main reason I went there was to tell them about Fred with the hope he would be prosecuted too," she says. "They told me they'd try, but that at the moment they had their hands full with Green."

Three months after the taping, Sarah's mother called her in hysterics. Her parents had been sent copies of the tapes. Key people all through the polygamist community had also received copies, including Fred. By the end of two weeks, all of Sarah's siblings had also received copies. "I called Ron Barton, and he told me Green's attorney got the tapes through discovery," says Sarah. "Green was his attorney's paralegal and made tapes for everyone. The A.G.'s office didn't bother to send them only the part about Green or file the tapes as protected discovery."

Remembering that Fred had warned her that if she ever told the secrets of the religion, she would be killed in blood atonement, Sarah was frantic. "I stumbled into my worst nightmare. All I could think of was how I was going to be killed," she says. "Then Fred's daughter called and told me that Fred called her to say he was going to take care of me. I flipped out."

Sarah phoned Tapestry Against Polygamy, who sent representatives with her and her sister to a meeting with Barton, Leavitt and Diana Hollis, an investigator with their office. "They were patronizing, telling us how they didn't think Tom [Green] would do that," says Sarah. "Then Leavitt went into his bullshit rhetoric about us being pioneers by giving them this information, and how he was a pioneer when he was on his Mormon mission as a white boy surrounded by black people in New York."

Reminding them that their lives were in danger, the women asked for a home alarm system and a gun. Barton and Leavitt refused the gun and mentioned that there might be some agency that could help with an alarm system. "Leavitt told us we could tie a red scarf over our front door to alert police passing by," she says, adding, "I'd be long dead before that." Later, Sarah read in the newspaper that Leavitt bought a gun for himself due to threats he received while prosecuting Green.

At the end of the meeting, Hollis offered to give the women her phone number. "She said she didn't like to give her number out, but we could have it if we felt we needed to talk," says Sarah. "I don't know if she realized what she was saying. They just gave our phone numbers out."

The horror of what Leavitt and Barton allowed to happen after so much effort to create a new life was more than Sarah could take. The self-medicating ways from her Hanna past were a familiar way to cope. "I started drinking until I had a complete breakdown and was taken to the hospital," she says. "They considered putting me on the psych ward, but instead I was sent to a rehabilitation program."

Under a doctor's care, Sarah went back to work and school for a while but the difficulty of remaining sober has hindered much of her progress. She doesn't kid herself into thinking she's out of danger. "My dream is to leave Utah and not be found," she says. "Fred believes it's not murder if it's God-ordained."

The only fictitious name in this story is Mack.

EPILOGUE

Progress is being made in terms of enacting laws to protect girls from being forced or lured into polygamy and enforcing existing laws. In 1999, the Utah legislature, at the behest of Tapestry Against Polygamy, changed the age when girls can legally marry from 14 to 16 years. In 2003, the Utah legislature made it a second degree felony for anyone to marry a girl under the age of 18 in an illegal marriage and a third degree felony for parents to allow such a marriage of their own child. Again, this legislation was spearheaded by Tapestry. Yet some Utah state leaders have indicated that they would like to make polygamy a misdemeanor rather than a felony.

In May, 2004, Arizona Governor Janet Napolitano signed into law a bill modeled after a Utah law making it a felony for a married adult to marry a child. Other provisions hold parents responsible for forced marriages of their children.

In terms of prosecution in Utah, since Utah Attorney General Mark Shurtleff took office in January 2001, prosecutions of polygamists in Utah have come about only through the work of Ron Barton and investigators in his office. Barton's learning curve has greatly improved along with a zeal to seek justice, while Shurtleff has remained in the middle, playing politics on both sides of the issue. In July 2004, Barton was assigned to another area of work and replaced by Jim Hill. The Utah Guardian ad Litem's office has also recently made great strides in understanding the convoluted dynamics of polygamy and its harmful effects on children.

Prosecution of polygamy and offenses inherent to it is often thwarted by a sense that the problem is too widespread and involves too many people; effective prosecution is often confounded due to a lack of knowledge as to the dynamics of polygamous groups. As a result, Mormon and Christian fundamentalist polygamist religions and communities continue to thrive and grow with very little fear of prosecution for committing a felony, much less other crimes and egregious human and civil rights violations. When local officials turn on the heat, the polygamist groups move to areas where they believe they can convince locals that they are quiet, law-abiding people, as the FLDS has attempted to do in Eldorado, Texas, only to have their cover blown by former polygamists who recognized their presence and tactics and alerted officials.

The women who courageously have told their stories in this book did so with the hope that they will help others either in giving those in polygamy the courage to escape or in educating the public, including law enforcement, judges and social workers about dynamics of Bible-based polygamy and the abuses inherent in it.

GLOSSARY

Adam-Ondi-Ahman: The place in Daviess County, Missouri, believed by Mormons and Mormon fundamentalist polygamists to be the location of the biblical Garden of Eden, and the location where Adam "will come to visit his people ... as spoken of by Daniel the prophet." (D&C 116; see also D&C 78:15, 107:53, 117:8, 11) Mormons believe that Independence, Missouri, in Jackson County, is where the city of New Jerusalem will be built. (See D&C 84:1-4; see also D&C 57:1-3)

Apostolic United Brethren: Mormon fundamentalist polygamist religion led by Owen Allred centered in Bluffdale, Utah, with settlements in Pinesdale, Montana, and throughout Utah, Wyoming and Mexico.

Babylon: The evil world outside of the confines and safety of the religion or, in the case of an "independent," the confines of the family.

Baptism for the Dead: In the Mormon theology, it is believed that those who were not Mormon and are deceased are in "spirit prison." They can be released from "spirit prison" only after they accept the Mormon faith and have their ordinances done for them by proxy here on earth. Those in spirit prison will also be released when they rise in the resurrection and are assigned to one of the two lesser kingdoms if they do not accept the LDS gospel (see Celestial Kingdom). Some Mormon fundamentalist polygamists have the same practice.

Bishop: A male priesthood holder in the Mormon Church or in one of the Mormon fundamentalist polygamist churches. A bishop acts for his ward (parish) in the same way that a pastor or priest does but is a lay leader without formal training in a seminary.

Blood Atonement: The death of the sinner or enemy of the church to pay for his or her sins.

Book of Mormon: The book of scriptures believed by the Mormon Church and Mormon fundamentalist polygamists to be translated from ancient golden plates by Joseph Smith. The plates were believed to be buried in what is now the Hill Cumorah in Palmyra, New York, until Smith was told by the angel Moroni where they could be located. According to belief, Moroni was, in his mortal life, the same man who buried the plates, which are considered to be a record of an ancient people who arrived on this continent by boat during the time of the Bible to escape wickedness in Israel. Descendants of those people are believed to be the Native Americans of today. The golden plates are now believed to have been taken back to God (along with a sealed portion to be given to the saints later) by the angel Moroni.

Celestial Kingdom: In the Mormon religion, there is no heaven or hell. Instead, there are three degrees of heaven, the highest being the Celestial Kingdom, then the Terrestrial Kingdom followed by the Telestial Kingdom. The closest thing to hell is the Outer Darkness reserved for sons and daughters of Perdition (see below).

Celestial Marriage: A term for polygamy preferred by certain Mormon polygamous fundamentalists because it denotes the celestial origins of the belief. Other preferred terms are patriarchal marriage, plural marriage and The Principle. This is also a term used today for monogamous marriages performed in an LDS temple.

Church of the First Born: An elite group within The True and Living Church of Jesus Christ of Saints of the Last Days (TLC). They instituted a holy order of temple-endowed members after a description of the same from the early Mormon Church (Journal of Discourses 5:129). This organization within the church is made up of men deemed patriarchs-priests and kings and women deemed matriarchs-priestesses and queens.

Church of the First Born of the Fullness of Times: Mormon fundamentalist polygamist religion led by the LeBaron family with a settlement in Mexico and members in California.

Church of Jesus Christ of the United Order: Mormon fundamentalist polygamist religion led by Luis Gonzales located in Sacramento, California, and Jackson County, Missouri.

Church of the Lamb of God: Mormon fundamentalist polygamist religion led by Fred Collier located in Hanna, Utah, with some members in Mexico.

Cohab Hunts: After the Edmunds Tucker Act was passed in 1887, federal officials came to the Utah territory seeking information leading to the arrest of men cohabiting with more than one woman. Polygamists were called cohabs by the officials. Many Mormon men hid near or within their own homes in secret compartments or cellars.

Colorado City: The twin towns of Colorado City, Arizona, and Hildale, Utah, on the state border and once called Short Creek. Members of this community are made up of two "wards" of the Fundamentalist Church of Jesus Christ of Latter-day Saints.

Co-op: The short term for the Davis Cooperative Society in the Kingston group, the Kingston's version of the United Order. See United Order.

Council (The): The group of male priesthood leaders in fundamentalist Mormon polygamous religions reigning over their particular religious group or ward.

Creekers: The nickname given to the members of the Colorado City-Hildale town, so named because the community was once called Short Creek.

Curse (Mark) of Cain: The historic Mormon teaching that God gave descendants of Cain black skin (to set them apart from those who are "white and delightsome") due to their not being valiant in the pre-existence (pre-earth life). This belief kept anyone of black skin from being approached by proselytizing Mormons. If they joined on their own, men were kept from holding the priesthood and both men and women were kept from entering Mormon temples. This practice changed in 1978 with an Official Declaration added to The *Doctrine and Covenants*.

Davis Cooperative Society (Co-op): United Order under the Kingston group. See United Order.

Doctrine and Covenants (D & C): Volume of scriptures that are believed to be the revelations of God given to Mormon Church founder

Joseph Smith. Contains the revelation concerning the requirement to live polygamy (Section 132) and the Word of Wisdom.

Dumpster Diving: The practice of climbing into the large outside garbage bins at the back of grocery stores to find discarded food.

Endowments: "Worthy" adult members of the Mormon Church and Mormon fundamentalist polygamist churches are initiated through a ritual where they are given secret handshakes and phrases and sacred undergarments to wear continuously as well as knowledge and teachings not available to those who have not received their endowments. For Mormons, this is done in LDS temples all over the world. Mormon fundamentalist polygamists have temples or makeshift endowment houses for these same rites.

Fundamentalism: In this context, it is a movement stressing an active, uncompromising adherence to the basic principles and early beliefs of the Mormon Church.

Fundamentalist Church of Jesus Christ of Latter-day Saints: The Mormon fundamentalist polygamist religion led by Rulon Jeffs. Members make up the towns of Hildale, Utah, and Colorado City, Arizona. Members are also located in Creston and Bountiful, British Columbia, Canada.

Garments: Sacred white underwear with symbols over the nipples, the navel and knees. Only those who have been endowed in the Mormon temples or by fundamentalist priesthood members are allowed to wear these according to their respective religions. It is believed these undergarments protect the wearer from evil and harm; they are thus worn at all times next to the skin as a constant reminder to the wearer of the covenants and promises made during the endowment. Some members also subscribe to the Mormon folklore that garments physically protect the parts of the body they cover. Originally, the garments covered the body from wrist to ankle; now LDS Church members may wear modified garments that have cap sleeves and reach to the knee. Mormon fundamentalist polygamists continue to wear the original design of the early Mormon Church.

General Authorities: The highest male priesthood leaders in the Mormon hierarchy. They consist of the prophet and his two counselors who are part of The Council of 12. Also included are a Quorum of 70 additional priesthood leaders.

Gentile: In this context it refers to any person outside of the Mormon Church or a Mormon fundamentalist polygamist religion. This word has been co-opted due to the belief in being part of the house of Israel through the Book of Mormon.

Healing Blessing: Mormons and Mormon fundamentalists believe they have the power to heal through the male priesthood. "Consecrated oil" (olive oil that has been prayed over for this purpose) is poured on a sick individual's head, and two men call upon "Heavenly Father" to heal the person in Jesus' name.

Home Teachers: Mormon male priesthood members assigned to visit several families in each ward every month to inquire as to their spiritual and temporal needs, deliver a spiritual message and pray with the family.

Independents: Mormon polygamist fundamentalists within family units not associated with an organized religion or group. Within these families, the husband-father acts as the prophet-leader of his family members.

Journal of Discourses: A 26-volume set of books compiled from the speeches of early Mormon Church leaders. Not well known to mainstream Mormons.

Lamanites: According to the Book of Mormon, these are people who migrated to the American continent from Israel and whom, after arriving, God cursed with a dark skin due to their wickedness. This set them apart from their righteous relatives, the Nephites. According to Mormon belief, the Lamanites eventually killed all the Nephites in wars and are the ancestors of today's Native Americans. (The only exception are the legendary "Three Nephites" to whom Jesus granted immortality when he visited this continent after his resurrection.) It is believed that the last living mortal Nephite was Moroni who, before his death, buried a record of these people and events inscribed on golden plates in a hill. It is these plates that Joseph Smith is believed to have transcribed into the *Book of Mormon.* (This is a sticky point with Mormons today, who take the view that "dark skin" is not meant literally but metaphorically.)

Latter-day Church of Christ: Mormon fundamentalist polygamist religion led by Paul Kingston and located in Salt Lake City, Utah.

Latter-day Saint (LDS): A member of The Church of Jesus Christ of Latter-day Saints. Also known as a Mormon.

Law of Consecration: To consecrate (give) to God. To live the Law of Consecration is to fully pledge that all you have and all you do is for God and the building up of his Kingdom. It is more selfless than living the United Order (see below).

Manifesto: Believed by Mormons to have been the revelation from God given to then-prophet Wilford Woodruff informing him that it was time to end polygamy, thereby providing Mormon leaders with the requirement needed for Utah to be admitted to statehood.

Memory Gems: These are certain phrases that members of the Kingston group are required to repeat two times a day at the exact same time, all together, no matter where they are or what they are doing.

Mormon: The popularized name for a member of The Church of Jesus Christ of Latter-day Saints or for the church itself. Derived from the name of the *Book of Mormon*.

Multiple Probations: A TLC belief in reincarnation. For instance, they believe that their prophet, Jim Harmston, was Joseph Smith in one of his former "probations."

One Mighty and Strong: From the Mormon *Doctrine and Covenants*, (Section 85: 6-12) Refers to one who will be sent by God to "set in order the house of God." This is commonly interpreted to apply to the reestablishment of polygamy in Mormonism.

Patriarchal Christian Fellowship of God's Free Men and Women: The Christian polygamist religion led by Steven Butt through his Broken Shackles Ministry.

Patriarchal Hierarchy: The Mormon fundamentalist polygamist religion begun by Tom Green located in Green Haven, Utah.

Pearl of Great Price: Scriptures believed to be revealed to Joseph Smith by God, which include the Articles of Faith.

Plural Marriage: Another term for polygamy.

Polygamy: The popularized term for what is technically polygyny. In this context, it refers to the marriage of two or more women to one man.

"Polyg": Shorthand slang for a polygamist. Is often used an adjective, as in "polyg" clothes or "polyg" hair.

Poofer: Someone who is no longer in the community, as in, "Gone in a poof." Creeker kids often say someone became a poofer to explain why an individual disappears and is alleged by some to have been killed, left the group or been taken to the Mexican or Canadian settlements to be married.

Prayer in Robes: In the TLC church, adult members who have had their endowments are to pray as many as three times a day in sacred rooms of certain homes wearing their sacred robes over their sacred undergarments.

Priesthood: Authority given to all worthy males over the age of 12 in the Mormon Church and Mormon fundamentalist polygamist groups. Mormons believed that this line of authority was given to Joseph Smith by Peter, James and John who appeared in angel form. They further believe that Jesus Christ gave the priesthood to Peter, James and John; therefore, the priesthood is directly from Jesus.

Priesthood Adopted (adoption): From the early Mormon temple practice of adopting men into another man's celestial kingdom.

(The) Principle: Another word for polygamy, as in "Living the Principle."

Probations: See Multiple Probations.

Raised Arm to the Square: A posture or gesture made in temple ceremonies by Mormon and Mormon fundamentalists. The arm is extended outward to the side and bent at the elbow so that the hand and fingers are pointed upward. The gesture is used in LDS temple ceremonies by both men and women.

Release(d): To be allowed to leave a marriage (divorce only applies to a first marriage, since subsequent ones are not legal) or to be allowed or dismissed from a job, calling or stewardship.

Rescue Me Program: In the TLC religion, a woman who wants to leave a husband and family must go through the priesthood leader of the Rescue Me Program for a release from the marriage so she can be remarried.

Righteous Branch: The Mormon fundamentalist polygamist religion led by Gerald Peterson and located near Cedar City, Utah.

Sealed: A covenant that binds one to another for eternity

Seminary: Classes taught each weekday to Mormon youth in middle school and high school. Each year is dedicated to one of the four "standard works," which consist of the Bible, the *Book of Mormon*, the *Doctrine and Covenants* and the *Pearl of Great Price*. Mormon seminaries are typically located adjacent to all public middle and high schools in Utah.

Sister-wife: The term used to define the relationship between women who are married to the same man.

Son or Daughter of Perdition: A man or woman who has received the Holy Spirit and denied it, *knows* that Jesus is the Christ then rejects and denies him, crucifies him in his or her heart. Denying Christ after once having known him with surety is considered the gravest sin possible. (D&C 26:32-37) This person is considered next to Satan and will be cast into "outer darkness" for eternity. (There is no hell in Mormon doctrine other than figuratively speaking).

Stake: Like a diocese, a Mormon stake encompasses several Mormon wards in close geographical proximity. Led by a Stake President and his two counselors.

Stake High Council: Male priesthood members in the Mormon Church who make up a body of leaders who govern several wards.

Stewardship: What one has when one is "called on" by the prophet or other priesthood leaders to take on a job or oversee property, a person or a family.

Tapestry Against Polygamy: A group created by women who are former Mormon fundamentalist polygamists to help others escape polygamy and to educate and lobby for change in Utah.

Temple Recommend: A certification card given to "worthy," tithe paying adult members of the Mormon Church and required to enter into the temples.

The Gathering: The migration of people into Manti, Utah, to join the TLC religion.

Three Nephites: In Mormon doctrine, these men were among the 12 disciples of Christ when he visited the Americas (New World counterparts to the 12 disciples in Israel). Before ascending to heaven, Jesus granted each of the 12 his dearest desire. Nine requested they live "the age of man" and then be united with Jesus in his kingdom. The three remaining sought that, like John the Beloved, they be allowed to live on earth until Christ "come[s] in [his] glory." (3 Nephi 28:1, 4-13, in the *Book of Mormon*)

Time Wife: When a woman is married to a man for only the time they are on earth as opposed to being married for eternity.

Tithing: Members of the Mormon and Mormon fundamentalist religions pay ten percent of their earnings to the church.

Translated: Being translated is never having "tasted of death" when changed from a mortal to immortal state.

True and Living Church of Jesus Christ of Saints of the Last Days (TLC): The Mormon fundamentalist polygamist religion led by Jim Harmston in Manti, Utah.

United Effort Plan (UEP): The Colorado City group's version of the United Order. See below.

United Order: A communistic economic plan held as the ideal by the early Mormon Church and practiced in some early Mormon communities. Under this plan, all individual possessions, assets, financial and material goods were turned over to the church to be distributed according to need, not necessarily equally. (See D&C 51:3)

Universal Church of Jesus Christ: Mormon fundamentalist polygamist church led by Allen Herrod in Northern California and by Michael Labrecque, formerly in Fort Worth, Texas, now in Missouri.

Veil: There are two meanings for this word in the Mormon and Mormon fundamentalist religions. One is a reference to the literal separation between this world and the spirit world. Another is a reference to the curtain in the temples that serve as the symbolic separation between both worlds and is a part of temple ritual.

Ward: A group of members belonging to a church similar to a parish.

White Aprons: In the TLC church, the wearing of this color of apron during certain temple rites denotes special membership in the inner circle known as The Church of the First Born. As in the Mormon Church and other Mormon fundamentalist churches, all others wear green aprons during temple rites.

ABOUT THE ARTIST: JONELL EVANS

Oil paintings by Salt Lake City artist JoNell Evans illustrate the front and back covers of this book. Evans graduated from the University of Utah with a BFA in painting. Her works reproduced here are portions of a triptych entitled "Pre-Ordained," which appeared in the exhibit *Body Politics: An Artist's Journey in a Patriarchal Society* at Art Access Gallery in Salt Lake City, Utah (March-April, 2004). Below is a review of the exhibit.

Patriarchal Blessings

(from 3/19/04 review, reprinted with permission of *Salt Lake City Weekly*)

By Ann Poore

Artist JoNell Evans had so much invested in being a good girl. She wanted to please her family and live a normal life within the structure/ stricture of her church. But the life of wife, mother, and handmaiden to God that she was told she was preordained to live never really fit.

Over the course of her 20-year marriage, she became so silent and withdrawn she felt invisible. The year of her divorce was, in her own words, "momentous." After graduating from the University of Utah with a BFA, she had her name taken off the rolls of the Mormon Church. "I started a career," she said. "And I gradually began to build back some confidence."

Evans defines the patriarchy that dominated her early life as church, state and corporation, the major power entities "that made decisions about my life and my body."

Her triptych, "Pre-Ordained," represents three seminal events. Each panel has a female figure in stark white, surrounded by looming male figures in dark suits. Evans placed little pieces of tape by the men's feet—as they use in blocking stage productions—to show that men's roles are also restricted.

The first panel represents blessing day, with a baby held in a circle of men referred to as the "circle of love" within the Mormon Church. Years ago, Evans said, any man connected to the child could participate. Since there was no priesthood requirement, mothers began to ask if they could stand in this circle of love, too. The response was swift and final: No women allowed. "Now, all men must hold the priesthood, to stand in the circle," Evans said.

The center panel is the artist's baptism day, taken from a photo when she was 8. Her 16-year-old brother baptized her, something that still rankles. "My brother was able to cleanse me of all my sins! I was aware of male privilege even at that age."

The bride in the third panel is veiled, "symbolic of the many ways women continue to be veiled nonentities in this world."

ABOUT THE AUTHOR: ANDREA MOORE-EMMETT

Andrea Moore-Emmett is a native of Colorado who now lives in Salt Lake City, Utah. She speaks across the country concerning abuses against women and children within polygamy. Moore-Emmett is a prize-winning journalist and was the researcher for the two-hour documentary *Inside Polygamy*, aired on A&E and the BBC. Moore-Emmett is the recipient of five Utah Excellence in Journalism awards from the Society of Professional Journalists, including a 1st place Don Baker Investigative Reporting Award and a Leading Changes Award from the Utah Professional Chapter of Women in Communications. She serves as President of the Utah Chapter of the National Organization for Women (NOW).

READING GROUP GUIDE

Some of the women were able to escape polygamy, but after spending a fair amount of time away, went back to either the same situation or a new similar one. Why do you think this happened?

Some people and organizations believe the Bill of Rights protects citizens' rights to practice their religion freely, even when that includes polygamy. Do you agree or disagree with this? Why or why not?

The Church of Jesus Christ of Latter-day Saints once openly practiced polygamy, but since a proclamation in 1890 declaring that it should no longer be practiced in this life, now officially opposes its practice. What, if anything, does the Church now have to gain or lose by working with groups such as Tapestry or law enforcement agencies to stop the practice of polygamy in contemporary religious groups that cling to the teachings of the Church's early roots?

Are current-day polygamists practicing a religion, a cult, or sexual slavery? How do you differentiate?

How would you respond to a woman who says she is choosing, not being forced, to live in a polygamous marriage with other sister-wives?

What similarities, if any, do you see between the sister-wives in the book and women in polygamous relationships in other parts of the world, such as in many of the Arab countries?

Moore-Emmett describes troubling genetic, health, hygiene, and educational issues of many of the children born into polygamous families. How would you defend or prosecute a parent who asserts that his or her rights as a parent are being violated if a state's child protective services agency tries to intervene?

Is the practice of polygamy a religious issue or a civil rights issue? Explain.

If you believe girls and women are enslaved by polygamy, rather than choosing it by their own free will, describe the tactics and strategies used to enslave them. How and why do these work?

Do you see an end to the practice of polygamy? If so, how can it be stopped? If not, why not?

Do you see any possible benefits to women living in polygamous marriages? Explain.

Moore-Emmett described several situations when laws were clearly being violated by polygamous families, yet the police and courts refused to intervene. Why do you think this happens?

Underlying all of the stories in *God's Brothel* is religious belief. Does the practice of polygamy require a religious grounding? Why or why not?

• • •

Recommended companion books: *Under the Banner of Heaven*, by John Krakauer; *Leaving the Saints*, by Martha Beck (Random House, March, 2005)

Reading Group Guide by The Most Feminist Reading Group, Kitsap County, Washington, founded 1984. PO Box 4926, Bremerton, WA 98312